The Human Dimension in Education

The Human Dimension in Education

Essential Learning Theories and Their Impact on Teaching and Learning

Andrew P. Johnson

ROWMAN & LITTLEFIELD
Lanham • Boulder • New York • London

Published by Rowman & Littlefield
An imprint of The Rowman & Littlefield Publishing Group, Inc.
4501 Forbes Boulevard, Suite 200, Lanham, Maryland 20706
www.rowman.com

86-90 Paul Street, London EC2A 4NE, United Kingdom

British Library Cataloguing in Publication Information Available

Library of Congress Cataloging-in-Publication Data

Names: Johnson, Andrew P. (Andrew Paul), author.
Title: The human dimension in education : essential learning theories and
  their impact on teaching and learning / Andrew P. Johnson.
Description: Lanham, Maryland : Rowman & Littlefield, 2022. | Includes
  bibliographical references and index. | Summary: "This book describes
  essential theories and concepts related to human development, the human
  being, teaching, and learning"—Provided by publisher.
Identifiers: LCCN 2021045531 (print) | LCCN 2021045532 (ebook) | ISBN
  9781475852721 (cloth) | ISBN 9781475852738 (paperback) | ISBN
  9781475852745 (epub)
Subjects: LCSH: Education, Humanistic. | Education—Philosophy.
Classification: LCC LC1011 .J65 2022 (print) | LCC LC1011 (ebook) | DDC
  370.11/2—dc23/eng/20211012
LC record available at https://lccn.loc.gov/2021045531
LC ebook record available at https://lccn.loc.gov/2021045532

This book is dedicated to my brother, Thomas Johnson. A great brother, husband, and engineer, and an even better parent to two wonderful kids, Tilda and Frida.

Contents

Introduction

An Educational Psychology Book

This is an educational psychology book. Educational psychology is the study of learning and learners. This book is a companion to another educational psychology book, *Essential Learning Theories: Applications to Authentic Teaching Situations* (Johnson, 2019). That book focuses on learning. It describes four basic kinds of learning theories: neurological learning theories, behavioral learning theories, cognitive learning theories, and transformative learning theories (humanistic and holistic). It also explains how these theories are applied to classroom learning. This current book focuses on the learner. That is, the human being. We are, after all, human beings who are teaching other human beings in our classrooms. It makes sense then that we should understand these human entities involved in this very human endeavor of teaching and learning. That is the purpose behind this book.

THE RIGHT EDUCATIONAL PSYCHOLOGY BOOK

I have been teaching educational psychology courses in graduate and undergraduate teacher preparation programs for over 20 years. In this time, I have reviewed every college textbook published by every major publisher. I have been looking for just the right textbook to use with students who were new to the field of education. I have never found it.

I did, however, discover that most educational psychology books used for college educational psychology courses are essentially the same. Much of the same content is presented in each and in the same general order. In fact, you could study one educational psychology book and successfully pass an exam based on any of the other educational psychology books. The only real differences are that the concepts are described a little differently.

I also discovered two major problems with all the educational psychology books published by these other publishing companies. First, they are all ridiculously expensive. These educational psychology books have lots of pictures, colorful charts and graphs, glossy pages, three-inch margins, and lots of extra features (few of which students actually use). They also are usually 600 or more pages long and are 8½ inches by 11 inches. This makes them much more expensive to produce. But do all these expensive extra elements result in more student learning?

The second problem is that there is too much information. The concepts are described too densely. Now, a professor who has a large knowledge base related to learning theories and educational psychology can easily understand all the content in these other educational psychology books. As well, a classroom teacher with lots of teaching experience can easily make connections to the concepts being described. But a preservice teacher with a shallow and disjointed knowledge base related to teaching and learning and very little, if any, classroom experience has a hard time making meaningful connections to the concepts. It is because the basic ideas behind these concepts are often obscured by the overly descriptive writing and the academese used to explain the concepts. As a result, it makes it very difficult for preservice teachers to fully access these very important ideas.

THIS RIGHT EDUCATIONAL PSYCHOLOGY BOOK

In this educational psychology book and my previous educational psychology book, I have attempted to address the two problems above. The basic ideas behind these concepts are described as simply as possible. The chapters are kept as short as possible. As well, I have found a publisher (Rowman & Littlefield Education) that allows the book to be printed in simple black and white, thus keeping the cost of the book low.

In this educational psychology book you will also find some topics that are not contained in the other educational psychology textbooks. These topics include Abraham Maslow's and Carl Rogers's views on human development, self-actualization, peak experiences, and humanistic education; Sigmund Freud's structure of personality and ego defense mechanisms; intuition; an evolutionary perspective of emotions, poverty, disability and race; systemic racism; critical race theory; culturally responsive teaching; mental health; teacher reflection; and a complete discussion of teacher professionalism, dispositions, and attributes. These topics deserve attention and will move you forward in your understanding of the human beings whom you teach.

Finally, there are a variety of sources beyond this textbook that you can access for no cost. There are hundreds of instruction videos, podcasts, and short articles related to educational psychology, learning, and literacy on the sites below. Please use them to enhance your learning.

YouTube: http://www.youtube.com/c/DrAndyJohnson
Podcast: https://rss.com/podcasts/drandy/
LinkedIn: https://www.linkedin.com/in/reading/
Academia.edu: https://mnsu.academia.edu/AndrewJohnson
Website: www.teaching-reading.com

Part I

HUMAN DEVELOPMENT

Chapter One

Development of the Human Brain

The brain is our learning organ. This is where everything starts. A brief review is provided below.

THE BASICS: IT'S ALL ABOUT THE NEURONS

A neuron is a nerve cell within our brain and nervous system that specializes in sending and receiving signals or nerve impulses to other nerve, muscle, or gland cells. Each neuron is like a minicomputer that transmits and receives electrochemical signals in the form of nerve impulses. Each neuron can send up to 50,000 messages per minute. Multiply this by the 100 billion or so neurons in our brains and you begin to understand the power of this human brain computing device.

Stimulated Neurons

When stimuli in the external world are perceived, relevant sense organs send signals to various part of our brain where neurons are stimulated. Once stimulated, a signal in the form of an electrical impulse is sent down a long fiber of the individual neuron called an *axon*. At the end of the axon there is a gap that separates the neurons called a *synapse*. A synapse is the point of communication between one neuron and a neighboring neuron. Here the electrical impulse triggers a chemical release (*neurotransmitter*) that crosses the gap. The neurotransmitters are picked up on the other side of the gap by *neuroreceptors* found at the end of a shorter, branching fiber called a *dendrite*. The dendrite brings the signal up to the neuron. The signal then continues its journey down the axon to the next neuron and beyond.

Stimulated neurons automatically send and receive messages to and from all the surrounding or related neurons. As new neurons become linked up, *neural pathways* are created, existing pathways are strengthened, and more sophisticated webs or *neural networks* are formed. These neural networks facilitate the processing of new and related information. In other words, new learning and experiences create new and more expansive neural networks, making it easier to make connections with other new and related information and experiences. Thus, learning begets more learning. The more we learn, the easier it becomes to learn more.

Experience Matters

Our neural networks are also used to make sense of the world in which we live. That is, we use what is in our heads (our neural networks) to understand and interpret all that we encounter. Since these networks develop as a result of our experiences, and since we have all had different experiences, we all experience the world a bit differently. As a result, when we read a book, listen to a lecture or podcast, or observe phenomena, we all perceive it, understand it, and remember it differently.

Implicit biases. Understanding how neural networks are formed helps us understand implicit biases (see Chapter 21). *Implicit biases* are the unconscious attitudes, stereotypes, prejudices, and assumptions we hold about groups of people. *Implicit* means we are projecting traits on people or things without being aware of how the contents of our neural networks are influencing what we see and how we interpret it.

The Implicit Association Test (see Textbox 1.1) enables you to examine some of your implicit biases in a variety of areas including race, religion, disability, age, culture, sexual orientation, gender, weapons, and even skin tone. This test measures the speed at which you associate positive and negative words to targeted images. In the case of race, Black faces and White faces are used. Positive and negative words are presented. Words that are more closely associated with a target image enable the test-taker to respond more quickly than words not as closely associated. In other words, stronger neural connections enable you to link positive words more quickly to one type of target and negative words to another type of target. Take the test. It is very informative.

TEXTBOX 1.1. LINK FOR IMPLICIT ASSOCIATION TEST

Implicit Association Test
https://implicit.harvard.edu/implicit/takeatest.html

Differing views. Understanding neural networks helps us to understand how it is that people have such widely varying views on issues related to things like education, religion, and politics (Johnson, 2019). The differing experiences we have had, the people we have interacted with, the conversations of which we have been a part, the books we have read, and the media we have consumed have all contributed to our unique interconnected series of neural networks. This is why people of good character can have widely differing views on issues related to education, religion, or politics. Our views are shaped by our experiences.

This explains as well why, when talking to somebody with strongly held beliefs that may differ from yours, you cannot expect to change his or her point of view no matter how cogent or salient your arguments might be. Expansive, interconnected neural networks will not be reconfigured by a few facts. Instead, there is a natural impulse to initially discredit, reject, or explain away views that do not align with current ways of thinking. However, in education, we must be cognizant of this natural impulse as it does not enable our field to evolve. Rejecting ideas without consideration also does not enable us to evolve individually. By considering a variety of ideas, we are able to expand our neural networks and continue to evolve as both teachers and human beings.

DEVELOPMENT OF THE BRAIN

This section provides some basic information related to brain development.

Size Matters

First, size: The brain nearly triples in size from birth to age three (Ormrod, 2012). By the age of five, a child's brain is nearly the size of an adult's brain. From middle childhood until late adolescence and early adulthood, several parts of the brain continue to increase in size, including the frontal and temporal lobes, hippocampus, amygdala, and corpus callosum. These all play important roles in thinking and learning. The frontal lobe is especially significant because it plays an important role in planning, decision-making, impulse control, and self-regulation (Strauss et al., 2009). This part of the brain does not develop fully until early adulthood. This is why adolescents are sometimes prone to engaging in risky behaviors or making ill-advised decisions.

Neurons

At birth there are over 100 billion neurons in our brain; however, they are not yet fully developed or connected (Gazzaniga et al., 2002). After birth there is an explosion of new synapses created in a process called *synaptogenesis*. Here neurons grow new dendrites that begin connecting up with neighboring neurons to form new synapses. A synapse is the little space between neurons that is connected by nerve impulses.

As the neurons form synapses, they begin to take on specific specialized structures and functions. Based on interaction with the environment, some neurons are used repeatedly, thereby increasing the synapses and making the connections between related neurons stronger. This specialization occurs as a result of each child's unique interaction with their environment (Hinton et al., 2008). This enables the brain to adapt to each child's specific environment (more on this below). In other words, as the developing child acts upon the world, the world in turn acts upon the child in the form of new neural pathways and neural networks. As stated previously, learning actually changes the physical structure of the brain as new neural networks are formed. The term for this is *neural plasticity*. It refers to the brain's ability to organize and reorganize itself by forming new neural connections throughout one's life.

Pruning

Neurons that are unused gradually disintegrate and whither way. This process is known as *synaptic pruning*. Specialization and pruning enable humans to adapt to their particular environment. It is a way of making our brains more efficient and effective in dealing with the unique demands of its environment. For example, newborn children are able to perceive all the phonemic contrasts that occur in human languages. But within the first year, they can only perceive the phonemic contrasts within their own language. They become sensitive to the sounds within their own linguistic environment while gradually diminishing their ability to hear the phonemic contrasts found in other languages.

A Classic Experiment

Environment and interaction matter in brain development. In a classic experiment, mice were put in two different environments. In one environment, mazes and other types of stimulation were provided. In the second condition, mice were given no stimulation. They sat in cages with nothing to do. A comparison of the neural networks of the two groups of mice found significantly more neural connections in the mice with the stimulating environment versus those in the unstimulated environment.

The application here is that children need to have stimulation in their environments as well as human interaction during the critical years of birth through age five. This need not be super-stimulating environments. Indeed, too much stimulation may be just as disruptive as too little stimulation. Instead, children need conversation with adults and older children. They need books and a few things to play with. And, they need opportunities to play and just to mess about.

Myelination

The last thing to describe is myelination. The brain is not a finished organ at birth. A process called *myelination* begins before birth and generally continues into adolescence. The myelin sheath around the neuron's axon is similar to the rubber coating on the outside of an electric wire. The formation of this sheath around the axon is called myelination. Over time, it greatly speeds up the rate at which electrical impulses travel along the axon. Thus, myelination enhances the brain's capacity to process information and respond quickly and efficiently to stimuli encountered in the real world.

APPLICATION

Three big ideas:

1. Our experiences shape who we are and how we see the world in which we live. This helps us understand how it is that people can see, experience, and remember the same events so differently.
2. We use our neural networks to understand the world. Teachers can enhance new learning by connecting it to these neural networks. In other words, new knowledge should always be connected to things that children already know or have experienced.
3. The development of children's brains is enhanced by gentle stimulation in the form of play, adult interaction, and opportunities to mess around with things in their environment. These can play an important role in children's neurocognitive development.

Chapter Two

Cognitive Development
Jean Piaget

PIAGET'S THEORY OF COGNITIVE DEVELOPMENT

Swiss psychologist Jean Piaget's (1896–1980) theory of children's cognitive development has had tremendous impact on the field of education. Before Piaget, people thought children's brains functioned much the same as adult's brains. They just needed to be filled with raw knowledge and experience in order to function in an adult manner. Piaget demonstrated that our brains and mental functioning develop through a series of universal stages and that we think in distinctly different ways at each stage.

Some Basic Ideas About Learning

Children are active learners who naturally want to explore their environments and make sense of that which they encounter (Ormrod et al., 2020). As they do so, they encounter new phenomena. These phenomena are organized into *schemas* (Eggen & Kauchak, 2020). Schemas (sometimes called schemata) are like file folders in the head containing groups of similar knowledge and thinking. These file folders are used to make sense of the new phenomena. All the file folders (schemas) are organized into a cognitive structure. Staying with the analogy, a *cognitive structure* would be like a file cabinet in which the file folders are organized by content.

As children encounter new things, new schemas emerge and develop. As these schemas become more organized and complex, thinking becomes more sophisticated (Johnson, 2013). As stated in Chapter 1, this points to the importance of children's experiences and interaction with the physical and social world (Olsen & Hergenhan, 2009). These are both essential for cognitive development.

9

Assimilation and Accommodation

According to Piaget, learning occurs through assimilation and accommodation (Johnson, 2019). *Assimilation* is when we encounter new phenomena that correspond with our existing schemes. Here schemas are expanded. *Accommodation* is when new phenomena do not fit our existing schemas or when no related schemas exist. Existing schemas must then be restructured or new ones must be created. Learning requires both assimilation and accommodation. Assimilation occurs because new information is based on old information. That is, we use existing knowledge to understand and make sense of the new. Accommodation occurs because new information requires existing schemas to be reorganized or new schemas to be created.

As an example, a young child knows that all living things need air to live. The child learns that fish swim in the water and get oxygen from the water through their gills. This makes sense and fits with the child's experiences observing people catching fish at a lake. This is assimilation. Later, the child is told that a dolphin lives in the ocean but is not a fish. It is a mammal that breathes air like humans do. To incorporate this new knowledge, the child must restructure existing schemas. This is accommodation.

Equilibration

Equilibration is the constant striving for balance between new information and existing schemas. This is the motivating force behind all learning. Because of their natural curiosity, children constantly seek out and encounter new phenomena. This creates *disequilibrium*, a very dissatisfying mental state in which things do not quite make sense. Children seek to alter this dissatisfying state and move to a state of equilibrium through assimilation and accommodation. This constant state of movement from disequilibrium to equilibrium to disequilibrium and back to equilibrium is how children continue to learn and expand their cognitive structures. This in turn leads to more advanced understanding and the cycle of learning continues. This is how human beings expand their knowledge of the world in which they live.

PIAGET'S STAGES OF COGNITIVE DEVELOPMENT

According to Piaget, changes in thinking occur in four stages as children develop: (a) the sensorimotor stage, (b) the preoperational stage, (c) the concrete operational stage, and (d) the formal operational stage.

Sensorimotor Stage

The sensorimotor stage is from birth to approximately age two. Here children's early cognitive development is largely controlled by their senses and their ability to move—hence the label *sensorimotor*. An important cognitive milestone at this stage is *object permanence*. This is the realization that something not immediately available to one's senses still exists. At this stage, children gradually develop the ability to form *mental representations* of sensory objects (mother's face, doll, pet dog) that they can carry in their developing memory and can access as needed. This new cognitive function is known as *representational thinking*.

As this ability grows, children begin to realize that if you put a ball behind your back it still exists. Likewise, children's ability to move and thereby to view the world from different perspectives enhances their cognitive development. The greater their ability to move, the greater their ability to see the world from different perspectives: front and back, above and below, and near and far. This ability to move also allows them to seek out hidden objects whose representations now exist in memory.

Interiorization begins to occur at this stage as well. Here children become less dependent on their physical environment for thinking and responding and more dependent on internal cognitive structures.

Another major accomplishment that takes place at the sensorimotor stage is the ability to carry out goal-directed actions. This is the ability to contemplate and complete more than one action in order to reach a goal. For example, if a child cannot open a cardboard box to get to a cookie, he or she might seek some sort of tool to open the lid or tear the box. This represents the change in thinking that occurs during this stage.

Preoperational Stage

The preoperational stage is from approximately age two to seven. Piaget described an *operation* as an action carried out through logical thinking. Having acquired representational thinking (see above), preoperational thinking is the stage just before children are able to use formalized logic. Here vocabularies generally expand from 200 to around 2,000 or more words.

Although children are learning language and language rules, they do not yet understand logical relationships and they cannot mentally manipulate information. This stage is marked by *irreversible thinking*, that is, the ability to think in one only direction (they can not reverse an operation). For example, if a child sees somebody flatten a ball of dough, the child does not realize that the dough can be made into a ball again. Preoperational children are also highly *egocentric* in that they have a hard time taking another person's point of view. For example, they have difficulty in understanding that Pete is my dad, but he is also Andy's brother. They still see the world only in terms of themselves.

A major learning task that occurs near the end of this stage is *conservation.* This is the stage at which children begin to understand that even though the appearance or characteristics of an object may change, the amount or volume stays the same. They realize, for example, that if you have two equal balls of cookie dough and flatten one, the two balls still contain the same amount of cookie dough. Or, if you break one ball of cookie dough into four big pieces and a similar ball into 20 little pieces, they still contain the same amount. Or, if one row of 20 M&Ms is spaced close together and another row of 20 M&Ms is spaced further apart, they still contain the same number. Children generally achieve this realization around age six or seven.

Concrete Operational Stage

The concrete operational stage is approximately age seven to eleven. This stage is marked by the start of logical thinking. For example, irreversible thinking begins to give way to reversible thinking. That is, children are now able to understand that that $3 - 2 = 1$ is the reverse of $2 + 1 = 3$. However, all thinking must be very concrete and based in the present. When introducing numbers and the concepts of addition and subtraction, children in preschool through grade one should be given chips, buttons, or other concrete counters to see and manipulate. Likewise, all science instruction should be as hands-on and active as possible (learning by doing versus learning by listening, watching, or reading).

Children at this stage are also beginning to understand if/then thinking. If X happens then Y will happen. For example, if I put too many blocks on the pile, then it will tip over. If the tinfoil boat has high sides, then it will hold more pennies. If an animal has certain characteristics, then it is an amphibian. However, when learning to think in logical sequences, the objects of thought or some physical representation of them should always be present. Remember, this is the very beginning of their system of logical thinking.

A particular type of thinking that develops at this stage is *classification.* In the previous (preoperational) stage, children could group objects only according to one attribute at a time (color, size, etc). Concrete-operational children, however, can begin to group things based on a number of different attributes.

For example, given a description of felines, they can put tigers, panthers, and house cats in one group, and foxes, wolves, and pugs in another group.

However, children at this stage are still unable to think abstractly. For example, given a list of storybook and movie characters, children at this stage would have hard time putting them in a group according to which are heroes and which are villains. They would also have a hard time deciding which actions represent freedom or which rules illustrate democracy. This is because children at this stage are still highly dependent on perceptual differences in classifying objects and experiences.

Formal Operational Stage

The formal operational stage is approximately age eleven on. At this stage children begin to acquire the ability to think abstractly, that is, to develop and manipulate symbols and to generalize to similar situations. For example, they are able to make the following mental operations: If $A > B$ and $B > C$, then $A > C$. Or they can make analogies such as big is to little as slow is to (a) wide, (b) turtle, or (c) fast. Or they can even create abstract metaphors.

Children also begin to develop the ability to use more advanced deductive thinking, inductive thinking (see below), and hypothetical reasoning (if/then). Learning these types of formal operations can be enhanced through the use of thinking skill lessons (see Chapter 14). A thinking skill is a cognitive process broken down into steps and taught explicitly. For example, *inductive analysis* is a cognitive process whereby one imposes order on a field by identifying and grouping common themes or patterns. The steps are as follows: (a) look at the whole; (b) identify reoccurring items, themes, or patterns; (c) arrange into groups or categories; and (d) describe the whole in terms of groups. To enhance students' ability to use this type of thinking, the steps would be taught explicitly using direction instruction. This thinking skill could then be used in a lesson or as post-reading activity.

To illustrate, in her sixth-grade reading class, Ms. Gomez's students were reading *Bridge to Terabithia* by Katherine Paterson (1977). At the end of the book, she had her students generate a list of interesting or important events that happened in the book. These were listed on the board. Students then moved into small groups, put the events into categories, and described the book in terms of the categories and the number of events in each category. Each group then used these same categories to compare *Bridge to Terabithia* to *Hatchet* by Gary Paulsen (1986). Graphs were used to make the comparison.

TWO BIG IDEAS

Two big ideas based on Piaget's theory are described here:

Developmentally Appropriate Practice

Developmentally appropriate practice is when teaching is aligned with children's developmental level and how they best learn. The National Association for the Education of Young Children has described 12 principles of child development and learning (NAEYC, 2019):

1. All areas of development and learning are important.
2. Learning and development follow sequences.
3. Development and learning proceed at varying rates.
4. Development and learning result from an interaction of maturation and experience.
5. Early experiences have profound effects on development and learning.
6. Development proceeds toward greater complexity, self-regulation, and symbolic or representational capacities.
7. Children develop best when they have secure relationships.
8. Development and learning occur in and are influenced by multiple social and cultural contexts.
9. Children learn in a variety of ways.
10. Play is an important vehicle for developing self-regulation and promoting language, cognition, and social competence.
11. Development and learning advance when children are challenged.
12. Children's experiences shape their motivation and approaches to learning.

Inquiry, Discovery, and Experiential Learning

Children as well as adolescents learn best by hands-on learning in which they are able to experiment, mess around, and discover skills and concepts (Ormrod, 2012). Pedagogical strategies to use would include discovery learning, problem-based learning, project learning, inquiry learning activities, and experiential learning (Johnson, 2017).

Chapter Three

From Outside to In

Lev Vygotsky

VYGOTSKY'S SOCIOCULTURAL THEORY

This chapter provides a brief description of Vygotsky's sociocultural theory of cognitive development. According to this theory, thinking begins externally on the social and cultural levels and is then internalized. In other words, thinking develops from outside to inside.

Language Is a Tool of Thought

Vygotsky described language as a tool of thought used to hold ideas, manipulate ideas, and transfer ideas. According to Vygotsky, language drives the development of children's thinking (Eggen & Kauchak, 2020). In other words, cognitive development occurs as children are exposed to the language around them. The language they hear represents the thought patterns of others. As they *internalize* these thought patterns, these thought patterns gradually evolve into their own ways of thinking. This again points to the importance of speaking with young children. What you say, how you say it, and how often you speak with children impacts their cognitive development.

The same internalization process occurs on a cultural level. As children grow, they are immersed in a particular culture with its vast array of symbols, values, and ways of viewing reality. They gradually take on the thought patterns of their culture. Thus, both social interaction and cultural immersion help to develop and shape children's ways of thinking. (Hence, the name sociocultural theory.)

Three Stages of Speech Development

Again, any thinking function of a child first appears externally on the social plane. It then becomes internalized and appears on the thinking plane. When the child speaks, this represents an externalization of thinking that had its origin on the social plane. Vygotsky described three stages of speech development.

First stage: Social or external speech. At this stage (birth to approximately age three), thinking is not related to speech at all. Instead, thinking is primarily in the form of images, emotions, and impressions. Speech only occurs on the social plane to express a desire ("Cookie!") or to convey simple emotions such as shouting or crying. At this stage, speech is merely a tool to make things happen in the external world.

Second stage: Egocentric speech. At this stage (approximately age three to seven), children think out loud or talk to themselves as they are doing something. For example, if Pat made a mistake as he was tying his shoe he might say, "Bad Pat." Called *egocentric speech*, it is used to guide behavior and help solve problems. It is an important part of the transition to inner speech and more sophisticated thinking.

Third stage: Inner speech. Inner speech is soundless speech or thought. Here speech becomes internalized and is used to guide thinking and behavior. This eventually leads to higher levels and more complex types of thinking, which in turn leads to more sophisticated usage of language. As well, thought and language become increasingly interdependent.

Developing Higher Mental Functions

Language, social interaction, and culture are important in the development of high-level mental functions (Ormrod et al., 2020). According to Vygotsky, we start out life with a set of lower mental functions that are genetically inherited (see Figure 3.1). These involve things such as reflexes, attention, and perception. These lower mental functions are largely controlled by the environment. In other words, cognition is generally limited to a human's response and reaction to environmental stimuli. As children interact with other humans, hear language, and are immersed in a culture, these lower mental functions develop and eventually evolve into higher mental functions. Again, thinking moves from outside to inside.

Lower Mental Functions		Higher Mental Functions
reflexes (sucking, grasping), attention, awareness, rudimentary conscious processes, association, elementary perception, visual memory.	social interaction language culture	memory, logical memory, planning, decision making, reasoning, operations or mental functions, semantic memory voluntary attention, willful
(There is no processing of incoming stimuli here.)		(There is much processing of incoming stimuli here.)

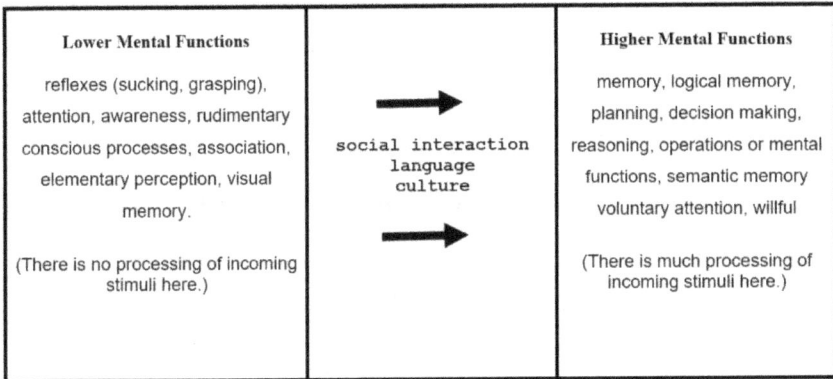

Figure 3.1.   Development and evolution of lower mental functions.

TEACHING AND LEARNING FROM OUTSIDE IN

When learning any type of skill or when learning new knowledge and concepts, humans of all ages and at all levels learn best if instruction takes place within the *zone of proximal development* (ZPD) and *scaffolding* is used.

Zone of Proximal Development and Scaffolding

The zone of proximal development (ZPD) is the level between a person's *independent level* and *frustration level.* The independent level is the level at which a person can perform a task easily without any help (see Figure 3.2). For example, Sally is reading at the third-grade level. Any reading material at the third-grade level would be at her independent level. The frustration level is the level at which a person cannot perform a task no matter how much help they might have. Reading a high school physics textbook would be a task that is at Sally's frustration level. Even with teacher support, she would not be able to do this. The zone of proximal development is the level just above the independent level in which a task might be accomplished with help. This help is called a scaffold.

Scaffolding in an educational context is the strategy of providing some sort of structure or support so students can complete a task that is a little above their independent level (within the ZPD). For example, Sally might be asked to read a book written at the fourth-grade level. An outline used as an advanced organizer would be an example of scaffolding. Here the teacher would go through this with Sally before reading. This would provide the support necessary (scaffolding) to enable Sally to read the text that is just above her independent level and within her zone of proximal development. Reading a text at her frustration level, even with scaffolding, would result in failure and frustration.

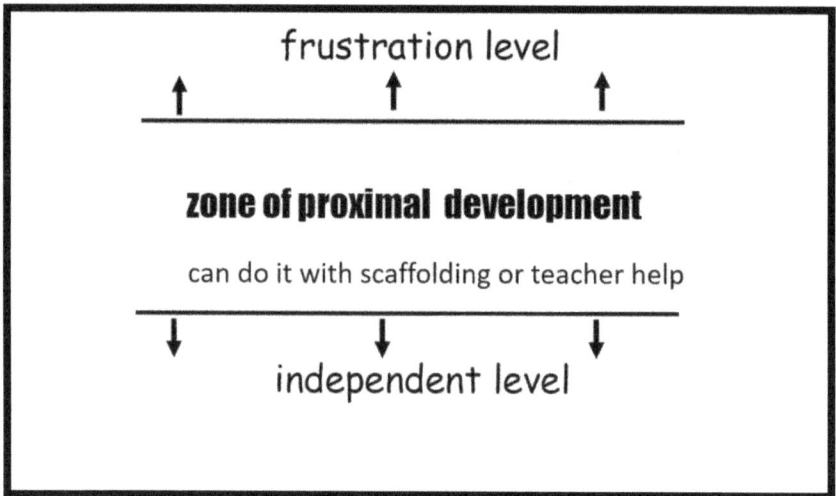

Figure 3.2.   Zone of proximal development.

Sadly, struggling readers are commonly asked to read textbooks that are above their independent reading level with no help or scaffolding. This puts them at a severe disadvantage for learning. Instead, there are many simple pre-reading strategies that can be used to enable all students to successfully read textbooks that might be a above their independent reading level (Johnson, 2017).

This is even more problematic for the 3% to 5% of students who are severely struggling readers (Johnson, 2021). Even with scaffolding they are often unable to read textbooks that are at their grade level. We do not want these severely struggling readers to fall behind conceptually. Because new learning is highly dependent on old learning, we want them to be exposed to the same concepts and vocabulary as other learners. Thus, for severely struggling readers, having access to audio recorded textbooks is an essential part of their accommodation.

Here is another example of scaffolding. Professor Johnson is teaching a complex theory to the students in his educational psychology course. The theory is new to most students. Rather than present the theory in its entirety, he presents just the basic elements, knowing that this will provide a scaffold to understand a more sophisticated version of the theory when it is encountered in another class later in their teacher education program.

Examples of Scaffolding

Scaffolding and the zone of proximal development are important concepts for success in any sort of teaching, whether it is in music, athletics, drama, forensics, business, math, or any other curriculum area. Here, you find out where students are at and then get out a little in front of them with some supports to help them succeed. It can apply to teaching a skill as well as to teaching concepts. Below three examples of scaffolding are presented. Each of these enables students to learn something that is slightly above their independent level but within their zone of proximal development.

- **Ms. Kim** is teaching double-digit addition to her second-grade math students. Her students understand the concept of addition, but they get a little mixed up when they have to line up the numbers. She writes the problem like this on the board: $23 + 35 = \_\_\_$. Then she uses the scaffold below to help her students understand where the numbers line up. As students grasp the concept, she uses less structure.

- **Coach Johnson** is teaching his wrestlers a complicated wrestling move that involves many different steps. First, he demonstrates the move so they can see what it looks like; however, providing just a verbal explanation would frustrate about 80% of them. Next he breaks the move into four steps and verbally guides them through each step together. ("Step one, put your foot on the outside of your opponent's foot. Step two, grab the ankle, etc.") He takes them through the move several times, gradually speeding up as he sees that they get it. Finally, Coach Johnson is able to say, "Practice five of them on your own with your wrestling buddy."

- **Ms. Ortiz** is teaching long division to her students. Just like Coach Johnson above, she demonstrates the strategy first, then hands out scratch paper (thinking paper), and verbally guides her students through each step as she also completes the problem on the board. ("Step one, set up the division column with your numbers. Step two, see how many times the dividing number [denominator] goes into the number being divided [numerator]. . . .") She provides less structure until she thinks students have got it. She then uses homework for students to practice what they have learned.

Figure 3.3.
Math problem.

BIG IDEAS

The following are ideas based on Vygotsky's sociocultural theory:

- Language is a tool of thought.
- Children internalize the language/thought patterns from their surrounding social context as well as the symbols, values, and ways of viewing reality from their cultural context. This internally drives their cognitive development.
- Speech and thinking occur in the following three stages: (1) social or external speech, (2) egocentric speech, and (3) inner speech. During this developmental progression, the focus moves from the expression of simple emotions or needs to self-directed speech, and finally to internalized speech that is used to guide thinking and behavior.
- Language, social interaction, and culture are essential vehicles for the development of higher-level mental functions.
- Teaching and learning are enhanced if instruction occurs within the zone of proximal development and scaffolding is used to support new learning.

Chapter Four

Language Acquisition and Development

Language acquisition was touched on briefly in the last chapter. This chapter provides a more in-depth examination of how humans acquire and develop their ability to use language.

LANGUAGE ACQUISITION

Language learning is a universal human function. People around the world, in different environments and with different abilities, seem to acquire their primary language in essentially the same sequence and the same way. This tells us that humans are hard-wired to learn language in some form (Chomsky, 1968).

Four Elements

There are four elements connected with language learning (Ormrod et al., 2020):

- *Semantics* refers to the meaning of language. Children learn that certain sounds, symbols, or movements of a hand and facial gestures mean something.
- *Syntax* refers to the rules for how the words, symbols, and movements are put together. For example, in human communication there is usually a thing word (noun) coupled with an action word (verb). Children learn that the types of words, the form of the word, and the order that they are used in make a difference.
- *Medium* refers to the form the language takes. Children learn to produce certain sounds, symbols, or movements to communicate.

- *Pragmatics* is the context in which the communication takes place, and the social rules around that communication. Children learn to communicate in different ways, in different contexts, with different people, and for different purposes.

LANGUAGE ACQUISITION IN FORMAL EDUCATION

Language learning is not confined to childhood. Language learning continues in varying forms throughout our lives as we enhance and refine our abilities to read, write, speak, listen, and think. When formal education begins, teachers can enhance students' language learning by addressing the four language learning elements within their curriculums.

Semantics. Here teachers focus on developing students' vocabulary and word knowledge. There are three reasons why this is important: First, word knowledge enhances reading fluency and comprehension (Bauman, 2009; Jennings et al., 2010). Second, vocabulary is strongly associated with concept learning (Blachowicz & Fisher, 2000). And third, words help us think (Stahl, 1999); they are tools of thought used to represent, manipulate, and extend our thinking (Vygotsky, 1962).

Syntax. Grammar is a study of how our language works. Learning to use certain conventions of grammar enables us to effectively create and transmit ideas from our heads out into the world through our writing and speaking. In learning to speak, children acquire the basic rules of grammar by (a) speaking and getting responses to their ideas, (b) hearing other more mature speakers, and (c) having incorrect grammar attended to in the context of their authentic speaking activities. The same approach should be used for grammar instruction in schools with both writing and speaking (Johnson, 2008). This means that grammar instruction must be short and explicit, and then practiced and reviewed in authentic writing and speaking experiences. In this sense, writing and speaking are skills to be developed, not content to be taught.

Medium. The medium is the form the language takes. Here you learn how to produce language (write and speak), and to receive language (read and listen). Instruction in reading and writing are recognized parts of formal education. Learning effective oral communication should also be included in a K–12 language arts curriculum. This can take many forms in a classroom, including small group speeches (Johnson, 2017), structured conversations, T-talks, and simply providing time and space for students to talk with each other (Johnson, 2019).

Pragmatics. This refers to how and when to use differing communication styles. Not only the type of communication used, but the form. For example, when is it effective and appropriate to use email, text, and other media? When is phone or personal communication more effective and appropriate? What forms should these take? How does your communication style differ from one situation to the next?

One aspect of this pragmatic element is illustrated in *culturally responsive teaching* (CRT). Culturally responsive teaching builds on students' culture, ways of speaking, art, and perspective as the basis for teaching (Cruz et al., 2020). However, effective teachers then help students understand and navigate cultural norms for communication (Johnson, 2022). Here they are taught how and when to code switch. That is, they learn when it is and is not appropriate to use the various types of language and writing styles (Irizarry, 2017) (see Chapter 21).

THE BEGINNING

So let us start at the beginning. A phoneme is the smallest unit of sound within a word. There are approximately 200 different phonemes or individual sounds in all human languages around the world. In the English language there are 44. As described in Chapter 1, at birth, humans can hear all 200 phonemes but eventually, through *synaptic pruning*, children are able to hear only phonemes from their environment. Synaptic pruning is the natural process in which unused neurons and neural connections in the developing brain are eliminated. Young children thus become "hardwired" to hear the sounds in their own environment while losing the ability to hear the other phonemes (Werker & Tees, 1999). This increases the efficiency of the needed neural transmissions, thus enabling the brain to adapt to its environment.

Words

In the first months of life, young children are learning simple associations or the names of things. Around the ages of 6 to 7½ months children appear to recognize that repeated sounds mean something (Gerrig & Zimbardo, 2008). Once they recognize the connection between sounds and experiences, word learning begins. It is common for children to learn several word-object associations at or before the age of 9 months (Bergelson & Swingley, 2012). Between the ages of 18 months and 6 years there is a rapid explosion in word learning.

Stages

There are five stages of language acquisition:

1. Cooing. From birth to 1 month, infants are essentially eating, sleeping, and crying. From 1 to 4 months, they begin to explore intonational patterns. At this age, they can still discriminate between all human phonemes. However, through the process of synaptic pruning (see above) infants begin to lose this ability between 6 to 12 months.

2. Babbling. Babbling occurs between 5 and 12 months. At this stage, infants' babbling begins to take on the characteristics of language in their environment. Infants who are deaf use ASL as their primary babble language.

3. One-word utterances. One-word utterances occur between 9 to 18 months. Here infants make sounds that are related to meaning. The first words are usually nouns (for example, "cookie"). During this stage, their vocabulary increases from 3 words to approximately 100 words.

4. Two-word utterances and telegraphic speech. Between 18 and 24 months, young children begin to combine single words to form two-word utterances. From 24 to 30 months, mini sentences called telegraphic speech are formed. This is the beginning of syntactic knowledge. By the age of 2 most children know approximately 300 words. This more than triples in the next year so that by age 3, most children knowns approximately 1,000 words.

5. Basic adult sentence structure. By age 4, most young children have acquired the foundations of adult syntax and language. By the age of 10, children's language is fundamentally the same as an adult's (but with far fewer words, of course).

WORD LEARNING

Learning words is especially important for young children. Children's vocabulary entering first grade is the best predictor of reading comprehension at the end of second and third grade (Perfetti & Stafura, 2014). Children who have been exposed to lots of books, who have had a variety of experiences, and who interact with adults using rich vocabularies enter first grade well prepared to learn to read and write. However, children coming from impoverished backgrounds often have not had these exposures and experiences. This makes literacy learning much more difficult when they enter first grade. This points to the importance of high-quality pre-K education (vs. childcare or daycare), where children will be able to enrich their vocabularies and have a variety of experiences with words.

Once children enter school, they learn between 3,000 and 4,000 words a year (Graves & Silverman, 2011). By the end of elementary school, they know approximately 25,000 and by the end of high school approximately 50,000 to 80,000 words (Harp & Brewer, 2005). These words are not learned from vocabulary worksheets or by writing down definitions from a dictionary. The vast majority of the words in our vocabularies are learned naturally, by encountering them in meaningful contexts (Blachowicz & Fisher, 2006). This means that the more words children encounter in meaningful contexts, the more words they will learn (Lane & Allen, 2010). Thus, the most effective way to improve students' vocabulary is through wide reading and by immersing them in conversations, media, and instruction that utilizes a rich tapestry of words and concepts.

Word Knowledge and Vocabularies

Words are known at varying levels. At the lowest level we have a sense of what a word might be related to. At the next level we understand a word when it is seen or heard in the context of a sentence. At the highest level we fully understand the word in all dimensions, we can generate our own definitions, and we can use the word in many contexts. These levels of word knowledge help us understand four different types of vocabularies (Johnson, 2008):

- Our *listening vocabulary* consists of the words that we hear and understand in conversations. We understand more words in context than we are able to use.
- Our *speaking vocabulary* consists of the words we use in formal and information conversations.
- Our *reading vocabulary* consists of the words we are able to recognize as we read. Most children enter school with very few words in their reading vocabulary. As they develop word recognition skills this number increases rapidly. To the greatest extent possible, the words that emergent and beginning readers encounter in text should be words that they already know.
- Our *writing vocabulary* consists of the words we use to express ourselves in written form. This is smaller than our reading vocabulary. However, once we have fully developed our word recognition skills, our receiving vocabularies (listening and reading) are fairly similar, as are our transmission vocabularies (speaking and writing).

LANGUAGE LEARNING AND READING INSTRUCTION

Lexicon or mental lexicon is the term used for your mental store of words and information about words. It is the diction in your head containing semantic information (meaning), syntactic information (how words are used), and word forms (sounds and letter patterns). Your mental lexicon is highly organized around meaning. That means that in your head (your neural networks), words are organized and stored around words with similar meanings or associations. For example, the word "cat" is associated with other cat-related words. When you hear the word "cat" your brain automatically activates neural connections with cat-related things, such as "paw," "kitty," or "pet." Connections to non-cat-related things such as "wrench" are not activated.

To illustrate, let us imagine you are a subject in a psychology experiment. Here you are shown the word "cat" and asked to click a button when cat-related words appeared on a screen. Your response times are measured. You are then shown the word "cat" and asked to click a button when non-cat-related words appeared on the screen. Your response times are again measured. The response time for cat-related words would be microseconds quicker than for non-cat-related words. This is because words stored more closely together in your neural networks are more readily accessed. This is a typical priming experiment.

What does this have to do with reading instruction? Again, words are organized and stored in our head around meaning. They are not stored around letter patterns. When we hear the word "cat" we do not associate it with short /a/ words or words that begin with the letter /c/. Thus, in beginning reading instruction, some letter-sound (phonics) instruction is necessary to enable students to recognize words in print. That is, to make the connect between the squiggly shapes on the page, sounds, and the concept of "cat" in their heads. However, an overemphasis on phonics instruction can impede students' ability to recognize words and create meaning with print. This is because the focus is on letters and not on meaning. Expert readers use very few letter clues to recognize the words they are reading (Johnson, 2021). They rely more on the top-down flow of information that occurs during the reading process.

Top-Down Flow

When you perceive words on the page, this information goes from your eyes to a part of your brain known as the thalamus. One of the functions of the thalamus is to act as a relay station, sending incoming sensory information to the appropriate parts of the brain. When reading, sensory information taken in from the page goes to the thalamus, and then up to the cortex. Right now, as you are reading this page, this is exactly what is happening. What you probably did not know, however, is that almost 10 times more information is flowing from your cortex down to the thalamus than from your thalamus up to your cortex (Johnson, 2021). There is a massive top-down flow of information whenever we encounter words on the page. We are using what is in our head to make sense of what is on the page.

This top-down flow of information is evident in priming studies that show that participants are able to recognize letters more quickly when they are found within real words than they can when they are within nonsense words or a random cluster of letters (Straus, 2005). We can also recognize words more quickly when they are found within sentences than we can when they are presented in isolation (Fries, 2008). Also, you will notice that when you already know a lot about a topic, you are able to read much faster and with much greater comprehension than you do when you read topics about which you know little (Weaver, 2009). This is all evidence of the top-down flow of information that takes place whenever we encounter words in text (or any other context).

This also points to the absurdity of some types of reading assessments (such as DIBELS) that ask students to identify nonsense words and lists of words in isolate. These types of tasks have little to do with creating meaning with print (reading). Since these words are removed from any meaningful context, students are not able to use background information, semantics (the context of the sentence), or syntax (grammar and word order). Instead, they are just responding to stimuli.

To illustrate this top-down flow, read Textbox 4.1 out loud as fast as you can.

TEXTBOX 4.1. A PARAGRAPH ABOUT WORDS

Contexts many in word the use can we and definitions own our generate can we dimensions all in word the understand fully we level highest the at. Sentence a of context the in heard or seen is it when word a understand we level next the at. To related be might word a what of sense a have we level lowest the at. Levels varying at known are words. Word a know to mean it does what but?

You most likely read the paragraph in a very choppy, stilted manner with spaces between each word. You probably sounded very much like a struggling reader. Your eyeballs probably focused on only one or two words at a time. They did not move in a smooth line. Neither did they skip any words.

Now read Textbox 4.2 out loud as fast as you can.

TEXTBOX 4.2. THE SAME PARAGRAPH ABOUT WORDS

But what does it mean to know a word? Words are known at varying levels. At the lowest level we have a sense of what a word might be related to. At the next level we understand a word when it is seen or heard in the context of a sentence. At the highest level we fully understand the word in all dimensions, we can generate our own definitions, and we can use the word in many contexts.

Textbox 4.2 contains the exact same words as Textbox 4.1. The only difference was that the words in Textbox 4.1 were put in reverse order. Since Textbox 4.1 was meaningless, there was no top-down flow of information. You were deprived of the ability to use semantic and syntactic clues that would have enabled you to read smoothly. In contrast, with Textbox 4.2, you were able to use the information in your head. The sentences made sense. You most likely read the words with a smooth flow and paused slightly after each sentence. Your eyeballs most likely skimmed over the sentences, fixating on just two or three words in each sentence. You might have even substituted a similar word or two for one in the paragraph. These are all things that happen when one is reading for meaning instead of merely sounding out words.

LANGUAGE DEVELOPMENT THEORIES

This chapter ends with four common language learning theories. Remember, a theory is a way to explain a set of facts. Different theories explain different facts differently. These theories all explain some part of how language learning occurs.

Behaviorist View: Conditioning

According to this theory, children learn language through reinforcement. They are rewarded over time. For example, if they say "cookie" they eventually get a cookie. Children produce utterances and are rewarded by others through hugs, smiles, attention, or whatever the child is requesting. This is basic operant conditioning.

As well, children hear utterances associated with certain objects and events. Things that fire together, wire together. This means that neurons that get fired up at the same time become connected by neural pathways. The utterance and the object or event eventually become connected. This is the law of contiguity, a basis of classical conditioning.

Social Cognitive Perspective

The social cognitive perspective is based on the work of Alfred Bandura (Johnson, 2019). Here language is learned through modeling as children are immersed in the language. They observe others in social contexts using language in authentic speaking contexts. Observation and modeling are very natural ways of learning.

Social Cultural Theory

Similar to the social cognitive perspective, children observe and experience language being used around them. Children are immersed in a culture in which they encounter words and ways of thinking. These words and ways of thinking are gradually internalized.

Nativist Theory

Based largely on the work of Noam Chomsky (1968), language is seen as a universal human trait. All humans learn to speak, all languages share some basic structures, and all children move through a similar series of stages in learning language. Chomsky would say that all humans are naturally hard-wired to learn language. We all have a language acquisition device or a genetic predisposition to learn language processing skills. Exposure to language triggers this language acquisition device. However, environment still plays a major role in language learning.

The Correct One

So which language learning theory is correct? No single theory explains anything completely, and that includes language learning. Thus, like all theories, each is a little right and each is a little wrong. Looking at all of them helps you understand how humans acquire language. Knowing this also helps you design experiences, activities, and instruction to enable children to develop their abilities to read, write, speak, listen, and think.

Chapter Five

Toward a Psychology of Being

Abraham Maslow

Abraham Maslow (1908–1970) was among the earliest pioneers in humanistic psychology (sometimes referred to as growth psychology or third-wave psychology). This movement begin to emerge in the 1950s in response to the idea that humans were merely creatures driven by their subconscious (based on the work of Sigmund Freud and the psychoanalytic model), or were organisms conditioned to respond to internal and external stimuli (based on the work of B. F. Skinner and the behaviorist model). Instead, Maslow (as well as Carl Rogers, Erik Erikson, and Maria Montessori) saw humans as having a natural impulse toward fullness, health, healing, and growth (Maslow, 1968).

The three psychological concepts for which Maslow is most highly identified are (a) hierarchical structure of motivation, (b) self-actualization, and (c) peak experiences. Each of these is addressed below.

HIERARCHICAL STRUCTURE OF MOTIVATION

A Basic Understanding

Maslow's hierarchical structure of motivation is sometimes referred to as a *hierarchy of needs*. This is a rank order of things that humans require for healthy psychological development (see Figure 5.1). A very basic understanding of this hierarchy is that the needs at any lower rung of the pyramid in Figure 5.1 must be met before those of a higher rung can be addressed.

This hierarchy can help us understand why learning is more difficult for some students than others. These difficulties include things such as (a) coming to school hungry, (b) dealing with chronic and acute stress related to poverty and other factors, (c) lacking a sense of safety or belonging,

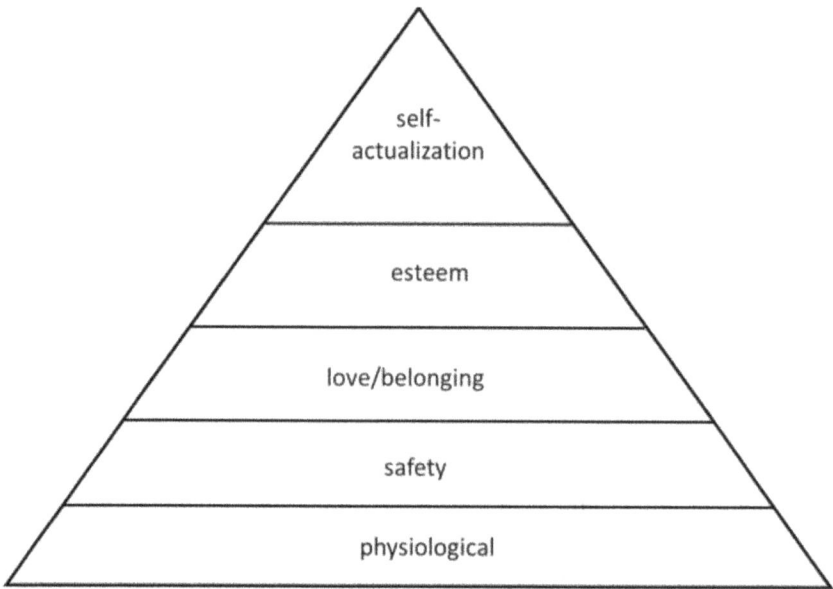

Figure 5.1. Basic understanding of Maslow's hierarchy of needs.

(d) being subjected to teasing and bullying, (e) not being able to develop friendships or feel a sense of classroom community, and (f) dealing with negative emotions, confidence, and self-esteem. These are all conditions related to the lower rungs of the pyramid. They all significantly impact learning, and as will be described in Chapter 20, they disproportionally affect students of color.

A Theory of Motivation

Maslow's hierarchy of needs in Figure 5.1 was originally part of his theory of motivation (Maslow, 1968). (Motivation will be addressed more fully in Chapters 23 and 24). This theory posits that humans are naturally motivated to fulfill low-level needs before they seek to address needs that are higher on the pyramid. A slight but important difference with the basic understanding above is that Maslow's focus was not on the needs; rather, it was on an individual's motivation to act based on these needs. Hence, it is called the theory of motivation (not the theory of needs). This natural motivational tendency promotes the survival of the biological and psychological human entity. This tendency is also aligned with an instinctive inner core that moves humans to naturally evolve to their highest state (see below).

Maslow identified two types of motivation: deficiency motivation (D-motivation) and being motivation (B-motivation).

Deficiency motivation. When a person perceives or believes there to be a deficiency related to (a) a physiological necessity, (b) safety, (c) belongingness/love, or (d) esteem, that person is motivated primarily to satisfy that need. This driving force is based on a lack of something and is what Maslow calls deficiency motivation or D-motivation. One is motivated primarily to satiate the desire or to get one's need met. This is low-level motivation. It focuses on getting something for oneself.

Being motivation. People whose low-level needs have been stabilized are naturally motivated to focus on higher-level needs or growth needs (see below). This type of motivation is what Maslow calls being motivation or B-motivation (see Textbox 5.1). Here one strives to be and become the highest version of oneself or to evolve to one's fullest state. These people are said to be self-actualizing. They are motivated to pursue optimal performance (peak experiences), to learn or discover (cognitive needs), to create or express (aesthetic needs), to develop their full potential as human beings (integration), or to improve the human condition or connect to something greater than themselves (transcendence). People who have deficiency needs can still achieve these self-actualizing tasks; however, the focus on lower-level needs detracts from these efforts.

TEXTBOX 5.1. MASLOW'S MOTIVATION THEORY

B-motivation, Being Motivation, Growth Needs, or Meta-Needs

(based on a desire to fully be and become)

5. Self-actualization = some or all of the following:
  a. Transcendence: help others, justice, equity, connect to something greater, love, interconnectedness
  b. Integration: personal growth, self-fulfillment, individuation, acceptance of one's nature or self
  c. Aesthetic needs: beauty, balance, form, to create, to express
  d. Cognitive needs: to know, understand, learn, discover, experiment
  e. Flow state: complete absorption, full immersion, optimal performance, in the zone, focus, compete, play

D-Motivation, Deficiency Motivation, Deficiency Needs

(based on a seeming lack of something)

4. Esteem needs = achievement, status, responsibility, reputation, self-esteem
3. Belongingness and love needs = to feel family affection, relationships, group identity, interpersonal intimacy
2. Safety needs = protection, security, stability, physical safety, quality of life, continuing income, protection of home, emotional safety
1. Biological and physical needs = food, air, water, warmth, sleep, clothing

Understanding

Again, Maslow's focus was not on the behaviors related to the needs in Text-box 5.1; rather, like Lawrence Kohlberg and Carol Gilligan (see Chapter 9) he was concerned with the motivation that prompted the behavior. In fact, looking only at behaviors can limit our understanding of the humans we encounter. This is because the same behavior can be displayed with completely different motivational needs.

To illustrate, let us imagine that Pat joined a group that worked to provide resources for local food pantries. If this was done for the purpose of giving back or helping others, this would be an example of B-motivation associated with self-actualization. However, if this same behavior was done to look good (esteem needs), to feel a connection to a group (belongingness), to establish physical or emotional safety that a group might provide (safety needs), or to have additional access to food resources (physical needs), it would be an example of D-motivation associated with a deficiency need.

Like all theories related to human beings, Maslow's theory of motivation should not be used to predict human behavior; instead, it should be used to help understand human behavior. Toward this end, this theory can provide insight as to why human beings sometimes do the things that they do. Here you must try to perceive the whole person, not just the behavior. You should ask, what type of need is the person seeking to fulfill or satiate by the behavior? Toward this end, the chart in Textbox 5.1 can be used to identify possible motivational forces.

People do not randomly or mindlessly act. They act based on one of the needs in Textbox 5.1. Therefore, when children display a negative behavior at home or school, it is always helpful to consider the possible deficiency need. You might even quietly ask the child, "What's going on?" In the same way, when a colleague, friend, or family member does something negative, destructive, or self-centered, it is again helpful to try to understand the deficiency that person might be trying to address. Why is this person doing this? What level of need is this person seeking to address with this behavior? How might this need be met in a constructive manner? By addressing the need first, the negative behavior is more likely to be diminished or discontinued.

This theory can also be used to help you understand yourself and enable you to set your intentions toward achieving higher ends. The questions you should always ask yourself when reflecting on intention and behaviors are these: What need am I trying to address by this action or behavior? What is my ultimate intention? Am I striving for money? Attention? Self-esteem? Or am I trying to make myself or the world a better place?

SELF-ACTUALIZATION

Self-actualization is the term used to describe the natural unfolding and realization of one's full potential. Put another way, within every acorn there is a mighty oak tree. To actualize is to enable the taproot to sprout from the acorn and the seedling to come forth and begin to grow to be the oak tree. Self-actualization is when the acorn recognizes the oak tree within, embraces oak-tree-ness, and begins the journey toward being and becoming an oak tree. But, as stated above, this occurs more readily when lower-level needs have been stabilized.

Self-actualization is not an end state. Rather, it is a state of being and becoming the highest version of yourself. Self-actualization is a continuing process that keeps you moving forward, and pushes you to fully evolve and develop your full potential in all dimensions. In this sense, people are not self-actualized, rather, they are self-actualizing. Appendix A contains Maslow's 15 traits of self-actualizing persons.

Self-Actualization Tasks

There are four tasks related to self-actualization: (a) discover and understand yourself, (b) express your inner core, (c) find your passion and act on it, and (d) discover your talents and strengths. Each of these is described here.

Discover and understand yourself. The first task is to separate yourself from parental expectations, societal norms, and cultural influences and to discover who you are and who you want to become. You not only discover who you are, but you embrace it. You are okay with who you are. You do not try to be or become something you are not. This task is prominent throughout childhood and intensifies during adolescence and early adulthood. It is also a task that must be addressed in different ways throughout our lives, meaning that at different transition points we must continue to reflect, reassess, and reidentify.

Express your inner core. This means to communicate the ideas, images, and feelings from your inner self in some form. This allows these ideas, images, and feelings to interact with other humans, and in so doing, creates a more dynamic and more richly defined sense of self. In the classroom, this can be done through poetry, writing, music, dance, the visual arts, and drama (Sylwester, 2000). It can also occur in individual and small-group discussions in which students are engaged in honest dialogue.

Find your passion and act on it. Here, you discover what is of extreme interest and has deep significance. You also identify what you love to do. Parents can help children here by (a) providing a variety of experiences, (b) reading a variety of books with their children, and (c) simply allowing their children to explore and mess about. Teachers can help by (a) exposing students to a wide variety of topics and activities, (b) providing a lot of books on a variety of topics in school and classroom libraries, and (c) creating the structure whereby students can explore and ultimately discover what is of interest to them.

The next step for parents and teachers is to allow and encourage students to act on their passions. In the classroom, this means designing learning experiences that include these passions. This freedom should occur in pre-school through graduate school. It also means providing spaces within the curriculum where students are able to choose study topics, writing topics, and books to read.

Discover your talents and strengths. Here, you identify what it is you are really good at and what you like to do (often these are the same). Too often, schools seem to spend an inordinate amount of time and resources identifying what students do not know and cannot do. This, of course, is detrimental to learning and to healthy emotional and intellectual development. Instead, a more logical, growth-oriented approach would be threefold: First, find out what students know and then design learning experiences that build on students' current knowledge. This is consistent with a constructivist approach to teaching. Second, identify students' strengths and use these to compensate for deficient areas. This does not mean that we do not remediate deficit areas; rather, it means that we also include instruction to help students use their strengths to compensate for these areas. And third, help students identify and develop their preferred ways of thinking, knowing, learning, and demonstrating their learning.

Nurturing the Acorn

Described below are five ways in which parents and teachers can help nurture the acorn. The word "child" is used here, but these ideas can be applied to children, students, and people of all ages.

UPR. First, use what Carl Rogers calls unconditional positive regard (UPR) (see Chapter 6). This is to accept the child for who she or he is regardless of the circumstance. This is different from accepting negative behavior. This also does not mean that there are not consequences for negative behavior. Instead, UPR means that you let the child know that you care for and still appreciate her or him. This is the soil and water that enables the acorn to sprout and the seedling to grow. This also means helping the child accept him or herself. Shaming used as an aversive conditioner to control behavior is antithetical to efforts here.

Safety. Second, provide physical, emotional, and social safety (to the degree that you can), which enables the child to explore and to feel free to be and become who he or she is.

Acceptance. Third, do not force expectations on the child. Do not try to make the child be or become something she or he is not. Instead, provide nurturance and support to allow the child to be and become who she or he is. By providing nurturance, acceptance, and a supportive environment, the true nature of the child will emerge.

Self-reflection. Fourth, in the classroom, include various kinds of self-reflective activities and experiences. These include activities such as writing, individual or small-group conversations, or simply pauses during the day to notice, feel, or listen. The arts can also be used here as both a means to express one's inner core and for intrapersonal exploration. Also, these sorts of self-reflective activities enable the child to recognize and begin to understand emotions and other motivational forces that operate below consciousness.

Respect for natural impulses. And fifth, listen to the oak tree within. Recognize and respect children's natural movement toward health and wholeness so they can begin to trust their inner guiding impulses. This also means we must allow children to begin to make choices.

PEAK EXPERIENCES

Maslow studied self-actualizing people to explore the potential range of human consciousness, among these was the *peak experience*. Peak experience is the term he used to indicate a special kind of human consciousness above normal consciousness that occurs when one is operating at his or her highest state (Maslow, 1971). Peak experiences are similar to Mihaly Csikszentmihalyi's concept of a flow state (Csikszentmihalyi, 1990). These are moments of heightened concentration that occur when one is totally absorbed in a task or completely immersed in an activity that fully challenges one's technical skills or imagination. Peak experiences can also trigger personal transformation toward higher stages (Harun et al., 1996).

Optimal State of Consciousness

Peak experiences are at an upper range of human consciousness. They are common among artists, musicians, scientists, writers, and athletes who, after years of mastering the skills of their domain, are able to obtain this optimal state of consciousness while engaged in a task within their domain. They are "in the zone." Professional athletes have said there were times when the game seemed to have slowed down and they could make decisions or see things three or four steps ahead. Peak experiences have also been experienced during meditation, prayer, or other contemplative practices. As well, this upper state of consciousness has been associated with moments of highest happiness and fulfillment related to human relationships. These could include a heightened experience of love between two people, the birth of a child or parenting, or an experience within a group of people working together. These are the moments that sometimes produce a state of consciousness where everything seems to flow. Performance is effortless. Time is distorted. Thinking and perception are enhanced.

Peak experiences are experienced in all domains and endeavors. They tend to occur when one is engaged in a task in which one has an extreme passion or interest, and in which there is a perfect balance between one's skill level and the level of challenge with the task (see Figure 5.2). As well, peak experiences can occur at any age. For example, a young child who is totally absorbed in some aspect of play, discovery, or exploration could be having such an experience. Or a student at any age can be fully engaged and immersed in a passion, be it a science project, music, drama, or some social event. They are totally absorbed in the moment or experience. Consciousness is changed. These instances can lead to peak experiences.

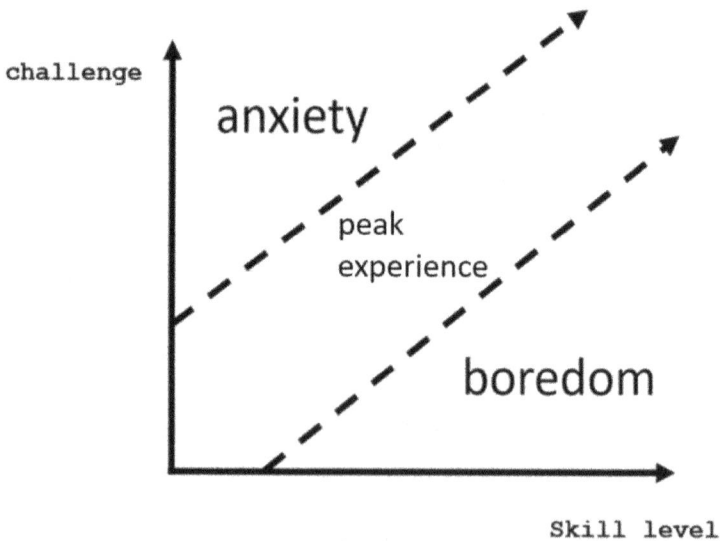

Figure 5.2. Balance for peak experiences.

The Goal of Education

What is the ultimate goal of education? Why does our society invest so many resources in educating our children? What is the ultimate purpose? Maslow (1971) stated that

> the function of education, the goal of education—the human goal, the humanistic goal, the goal so far as human beings are concerned—is ultimately the "self-actualization" of a person, the becoming fully human, the development of the fullest height that the human species can stand up to or that the particular individual can come to. In a less technical way, it is helping the person to become the best that he [sic] is able to become. (Maslow, 1971, pp. 168–69)

Chapter Six

Being and Becoming a Person

Carl Rogers

Like Maslow, Carl Rogers (1902–1987) was a humanistic psychologist who also described humans as naturally good and evolving entities. He pioneered a client-centered approach to psychotherapy that translated directly into a student-centered approach to teaching. This chapter describes some of his seminal ideas as they relate to human growth, teaching, and being a human being. As you read this chapter you will notice that these ideas are interconnected such that the borders between teaching and psychology are often indistinguishable. This is as it should be. Rogers believed that teaching, psychotherapy, and being a fully functioning person all came from the same place.

LIFE FORCE

Like Maslow, Rogers identified an instinctive inner core, or a self-actualizing tendency that moves people toward reaching their full potential (Rogers, 1961). He called this a life force. So why is it that some people do not reach their full potential? Short answer: Things get in the way. In other words, there is a distortion of this natural tendency. One of the roles, then, of a good teacher or therapist is to seek to understand the things that are in the way and to enable the person to remove them, or to get through, over, or around them. The important three words in the last sentence are *"enable the person."* Since humans are naturally evolving, self-healing entities, the role of a teacher and therapist does not take the form of external manipulation of any kind. It is not to tell the person what to do or how to think. Rather, it is to create the conditions that enable the individual to listen within, to find the answers that are already there.

Rogers's Five Characteristics of Fully Functioning Persons

Rogers used the term "fully functioning person" to denote a psychologically healthy personality. Five characteristics or traits of a fully functioning person are described here. And since humans are dynamic, evolving entities, these are traits that any person can cultivate.

1. **An openness to experience.** Fully functioning persons are not constrained by inhibiting worries of self-worth. As such, they are willing to try new things, have new experiences, and explore new ideas. Also, without the various defense mechanisms that come with trying to be something they are not, fully functioning persons are both willing and able to experience a wide range of emotions, both positive and negative.

2. **Existential living.** Fully functioning persons are able to live fully in the moment. They enjoy the present moment they are in rather than constantly looking forward to another moment in time. As well, fully functioning persons do not try to control or manipulate the moment or make the moment something it is not. They can therefore participate freely in the experiences that each moment brings. Also, they tend to see the world as it is rather than as they would like to see it.

3. **A trust in one's inner self.** Fully functioning persons trust their intuitive and emotional self to help them make decisions, solve problems, and understand reality. They use reason and knowledge as well as intuition and emotion when confronted with a problem or choice (see Chapter 12). In this sense, they trust and are able to use their whole self to guide them through life.

4. **A sense of freedom.** Fully functioning persons have fewer constraints or inhibitions than defensive persons because they are less worried about what other people might think of them. They also do not feel directed by current circumstance or influenced by past events. This provides a sense of freedom that in turn affords a greater choice of thought and actions. This also enables them to experiment with new ideas, to take risks, and to see possibilities instead of roadblocks and limitations.

5. **Creativity.** Creativity is a trait that often represents the highest degree of emotional health (May, 1975; Maslow, 1968; Rogers, 1961). Fully functioning people are original, inventive, and innovative. They are able to play with ideas, step outside the boundaries of perceived expectations, and think in new and innovative ways in order to solve problems or create products and performances.

Creativity

Rogers described three inner conditions necessary for creativity. These are not static attributes; rather, they are conditions that any person can develop. The first condition is openness to experience (see above).

The second condition is an internal locus of evaluation. Creative people strive primarily to produce what they believe to be good products and performances rather than what others believe these to be. They are not trying to please somebody else with their creations. Instead, they are motivated internally, relying on their own standard of evaluation. They create what is of aesthetic or pragmatic value to them.

The third condition is the ability to play with elements and concepts. Creative people have a certain childlike quality that invites them to mess around and explore new possibilities. What is believed to be true is not a limiting factor. Rather, creative people allow themselves to imagine a variety of possibilities regardless of their perceived likelihood or their basis in reality.

HUMANISTIC EDUCATION

Carl Rogers was a humanistic educator. Humanistic education defines learning not in terms of test scores, but in terms of personal growth and the development of each person's full potential. Growth and development occur here not just on an intellectual level, but also on an emotional, psychological, creative, social, and physical levels (DeCarvalho, 1991; Maslow, 1971; Morris, 1978; Rogers & Freiberg, 1994; Patterson, 1973). In this context, there are five goals of humanistic education (Johnson, 2019):

1. Facilitate the development of fully functioning, self-actualized human beings who have the capacity to nurture themselves, others, and their environment.
2. Instill a joy of learning and a desire to be lifelong learners.
3. Promote the discovery of each student's passions, special talents, and abilities.
4. Teach the knowledge and skills necessary for students to be good decision makers and effective problem solvers.
5. Enable students to be responsible world citizens who are able to contribute to democratic societies.

Good Teachers

From a humanistic perspective, a good teacher is not merely a technician manipulating students to predetermined outcomes. A good teacher does not simply follow a recipe, implement one-size-fits-all programs with "fidelity," or flawlessly perform a bunch of teaching techniques. From a humanistic perspective, a good teacher facilitates learning in furtherance of the five goals described above. Toward this end, Carl Rogers identified three traits necessary to be a good teacher. And just like the traits of fully functioning persons described earlier, these traits are not static entities. This means that any teacher can cultivate them.

1. Genuineness. There is congruence between your teaching self and your true self that creates genuineness and sincerity in what you do and say. You are genuine, honest, and sincere. You do not try to be or become something or somebody you are not. In this state you find that people generally appreciate us. This enables you to be a more powerful in your teaching. You are not trying to be a teacher; instead, you are being yourself who is teaching. When you do not have to spend the time and energy constructing facades, you can devote more time, energy, and passion to the act of teaching.

Early on in one's teaching career genuineness is a bit more difficult to achieve. But as one continues to grow as both a person and a teacher, the teaching self and the personal self become more closely aligned. This does not mean that you must lose your sense of self in your teaching. Far from it. It simply means that you teach from your authentic self. Here you are fully aligned with your values and your philosophy—and you are using your strengths and passions. This, of course, is predicated on first knowing exactly who you are.

2. Unconditional positive regard. You have unconditional positive regard for your students. This means you accept them, respect them, and value them for who they are unconditionally. Your acceptance of them is not conditional. This does not mean that you must accept negative behaviors. Instead, you realize that every student is of worth, even if their behavior may not be. You do not view them as something broken that needs to be fixed, or something deviant that needs to be corrected.

3. Understanding. You try to see the world as your students see it. You try to empathize with what your students might be feeling. You do not just focus on correcting behaviors or getting a desired behavioral response. You instead try to understand the circumstances and emotions behind behaviors. And you see the student in the context of the various systems: educational, political, economic, social, cultural, and racial.

FINAL WORD

Based on the work of Carl Rogers, there are two things that will enhance your ability to be an effective teacher: The first is to seek to cultivate the five traits of a fully functioning person described above. And the second is to form relationships with your students. Teaching starts with a relationship. Until then, you are simply a circus performer standing in front of your students performing pedagogical tricks.

Chapter Seven

A Pioneer of Modern Psychology
Sigmund Freud

Sigmund Freud (1856–1939) is considered to be one of the pioneers of modern psychology. His theory of personality states that (a) the human psyche (personality) has more than one aspect (see below) and (b) the unconscious mind can be highly influential in directing human behavior. His contribution to the field of psychology was in describing how impulses and ideas contained in the unconscious were sometimes blocked from becoming conscious (Tuckett, 2019). These blocks contributed to the suffering of his patients.

It is recognized that his ideas related to the impact of childhood sexuality on human development and personality are uncomfortable for many. These are not widely adopted today. But many of his other ideas still contribute to our understanding of the human entity. Thus, any book about understanding human beings should include some of Freud's ideas.

There are three things to keep in mind when evaluating Freud's theory of personality. First, theories are not meant to be permanent. Theories, by their very nature, are temporary structures used to explain a set of facts and to understand phenomena. As the facts change, the theories continue to evolve until they eventually become obsolete and are replaced by new theories. Second, Freud's thinking kept evolving throughout his lifetime. If he were still alive today it is most likely that his thinking would be much different than it was in the early 1900s. And third, theories (like Freud's) do not predict human behavior; they help us understand human behavior.

Three Levels of Consciousness

Consciousness is another term for awareness. Freud described three levels of awareness. The *conscious mind* contains all our thoughts, mental processes, memories, feelings, and perceptions of which we are aware. The *preconscious*

47

mind contains things that we could attend to and be aware of if we wanted to. These include memories that are easily retrieved. The *unconscious mind* contains the thoughts, feelings, impulses, and memories that are out of awareness. The unconscious mind also contains the memories and desires that (a) cause pain, anxiety, or discomfort; (b) conflict with one's idealized version of self; and (c) one finds unacceptable.

Freud's Structure of Personality

According to Freud's theory, the personality or psyche has three interacting elements: the id, the ego, and the superego. The *id* is the most primitive or instinctive part of the personality. It operates on the pleasure principle, seeking immediate gratification for some of your most basic inclinations, such as sex and aggression, regardless of societal restraints. These are irrational and impulsive forces that operate largely at the unconscious level.

The *superego* operates at both preconscious level and unconscious levels. Included here are your values, principles, and your idealized self. The superego is constantly striving for moral perfection. The superego is often constructed from parental influences as well as the cultural standards to which one is exposed. The superego acts as a form of moral conscience and is often at odds with the id.

The *ego* is the problem-solving part of the personality that seeks to mediate the impulses from the id (pleasure) with the demands of the superego. While the other two parts of the personality may be hidden (preconscious and unconscious), the ego operates at the conscious level. The ego enables you to meet the demands of the outer world (the reality principle) and at the same time work to satisfy the demands of the id in ways that are socially acceptable.

Freud's Ego Defense Mechanisms

Defense mechanisms, sometimes known as ego defenses, are the psychological strategies that are unconsciously enacted to protect you (or your ego) from the anxiety caused by unacceptable thoughts or feelings. In other words, they are things your unconscious mind uses to keep you feeling good about yourself. The problem with these mechanisms is that they also keep you from addressing underlying issues.

Ego defense mechanisms are used by all of us, at every age to varying degrees, and at different times in our lives. Understanding what these are enables us to understand ourselves, address our emotional roadblocks, and hold ourselves accountable for our behavior. They can also be used to help us understand others.

1. Repression. Repression is removing painful memories or unwanted ideas from consciousness. In other words, forgetting. Prompted by unconscious forces, these memories are pushed deep down into the unconscious part of your mind so that they are no longer accessible to the conscious mind.

2. Projection. Projection is when you attribute your own unacceptable thoughts and feelings to another person or group. In other words, you project your negative impulses outward, creating a false image on the projection recipient. For example, if you have feelings of hostility or inadequacy that might threaten your idealized sense of self, you accuse another person of being hostile or inadequate. This sort of projection is commonly used to justify prejudice and stereotyping of various groups.

3. Reaction formation. Here, unconscious impulses that you find unacceptable or threatening are replaced in your conscious mind by their opposite. You then repress these unwanted characteristics by acting in ways that totally contradict what you unconsciously feel. For example, if a person harbors a negative racial prejudice for a certain group, that person might block or conceal that prejudice by getting involved in antiracism causes or seeking to work with the group in some fashion.

4. Denial. Denial is our unconscious refusal to perceive painful facts or conditions by denying their existence. This can occur in situations such as abusive relationships, misdeeds of our children, or substance abuse of a family member. Denial enables the individual to escape the related thoughts or feelings that would be threatening to the idealized self or situation.

5. Intellectualization. Intellectualization is a defense mechanism in which painful or uncomfortable emotions are repressed by excessive intellectual activity. That is, you separate yourself from a highly charged emotional situation by describing it without emotion as if you were analyzing it from afar. For example, Pat's friend was extremely disrespectful to Pat in a public forum, but instead of addressing the incident and the accompanying emotions, Pat analyzed the disrespectful behavior, tried to identify possible causes for the behavior, and then evaluated possible solutions. Like other defense mechanisms, the extreme focus on facts, logic, and problem-solving might enable you to ignore the emotional impact, but it gets in the way of learning how to deal with difficult emotions.

6. Rationalization. Rationalization is when you attempt to justify negative or unacceptable behaviors using explanations that make them more favorable to you or others. It is a way to defend against feelings of guilt, maintain self-respect, and protect yourself from criticism or condemnation.

For example, a person who did not pay taxes might say, *"Everybody does this. It's just good business."*

7. Displacement. Displacement is when you relocate the strong feelings you have from one source to another. In other words, the cause of emotional distress occurs in one place while the reaction occurs in another. These reactions are usually transferred to a safer place or person. For example, a person who was treated poorly at work feels upset, but instead of reacting at work, that person displaces or transfers this feeling by becoming angry for no apparent reason with a significant other at home. Or a child who was bullied on the bus by older students might display extreme negative behavior in response to a teacher's request in the classroom.

8. Regression. Regression is when the present moment causes you to be overwhelmed by negative emotions so you to return or regress to an earlier stage of emotional or intellectual development where these dangers did not exist or where you were able to avoid confronting such feelings. For example, a young man was in a painful marriage that he did not know how fix. He found himself retreating to his parents' house and shooting hoops. In so doing, he was unconsciously trying to return to a time in his childhood before this kind of relationships existed in his life.

9. Compensation. Compensation is when you cover up feelings of inadequacy in one area by emphasizing your abilities in another. For example, a person who has very poor interpersonal skills that prevent him or her from forming relationships might compensate by becoming an overachiever in sports or academics. Or a student who constantly fails in the classroom might compensate by becoming a class clown. This points to the importance of helping all students find success in some aspect of learning. Students have a natural need to be successful or appear capable (see self-determination theory in Chapter 23). If they cannot find success in positive, school-related things, some students look to be successful with destructive non-school-related things such as drugs and alcohol, crime, or other damaging behaviors.

10. Identification. Identification is when you confuse your individual identity with the identity of someone else or a group. Here you unconsciously incorporate part or all of another person's personality, values, or beliefs into your own. It is common for children to take on some of the characteristics of parents or a favorite teacher and for adolescents to take on some the personality and values of an admired coach, famous athlete, or entertainer. It can happen as well with adults who incorporate some of the values and persona of admired political or religious figures and groups. Identification becomes a negative thing when the individual loses his or her personal identity in the process or if the values and beliefs being emulated are destructive.

TAKEAWAYS?

So what? What are we to take away from this chapter? What do we do with this all this stuff? Here are big ideas to think about:

1. **Being human means being unconscious.** There are dimensions to humans that go beyond the conscious mind. And according to Freud, what we see is just the tip of the iceberg. Much of the human personality is below consciousness. And although we are often not aware of it, the unconscious mind does impact us.

2. **Humans are wonderfully complex entities.** We are not simply two-dimensional creatures living in a Skinner-box reality, trying to earn rewards and avoid punishment. Also, humans are much more than a sum of their behaviors. Recognizing this is the first step in understanding the wonderfully complex human entities whom you encounter. It is also the first step in understanding yourself.

3. **Real education addresses the whole person.** Education is most impactful when it includes the unconscious element. As stated in an earlier chapter, this can be done through poetry, writing, music, dance, the visual arts, literature, and drama, and also in small-group discussions where students are engaged in honest dialogue, as well as biblio-exploration (see below).

4. **Biblio-exploration invites deeper understandings of self.** Biblio-exploration is a strategy in which narrative text or stories are used as a vehicle for students to examine and come to understand their own intrapersonal spaces. Stories enable readers to get inside the heads of characters and to make connections with their own feelings, memories, experiences, and images of which they may not be aware. It is by becoming aware of these motivating forces that one becomes free from their influence. This is a *catharsis*. In psychoanalytic terms, a catharsis is a sudden freeing of repressed material. When you are constrained by elements hidden within the unconscious mind you can be unconsciously directed by them. If we fully understand all aspects of ourselves, we are less likely to be pushed around by these unknown forces.

5. **Behaviors can be limiting in what they tell you.** Humans are not simply an accumulation of their behaviors. There are always complex motivating factors beyond the behavior. When negative behaviors are displayed in a classroom or other contexts, the focus should be on the behavior as well as what caused the behavior. You should not try to solve behavior problems simply by making the behavior go away. In other words, you cannot reward and punish the behavior away.

6. **People are not always aware of why they behave or react in certain ways.** As stated at the beginning of this chapter, much of human behavior arises out of the unconscious mind. Identifying some of the motivating forces behind our behaviors enables us to address our emotional roadblocks and hold ourselves accountable for our behavior.

Chapter Eight

Psychosocial Theory of Personal Development

Erik Erikson and James Marcia

This chapter examines two theories related to personal development: Erik Erickson's theory of psychosocial development and James Marcia's theory of identity development.

ERIK ERICKSON

Erik Erikson's (1902–1994) theory of psychosocial development states that the development of human personality occurs through a similar sequence of stages. But unlike Piaget's stages of development, his stages of development extend throughout our life. Also, like Maslow and Rogers, Erikson believed that humans were essentially good with a natural inclination to evolve to their highest state.

EIGHT STAGES IN THE LIFE CYCLE

Erikson's psychosocial theory of personal development describes eight stages that humans go through over the course of their lives. At each stage there is a *crisis* that must be resolved. The word "crisis," when used in this context, is a psychological task that must be accomplished or an issue that must be resolved in order for a person to take a significant step forward in his or her development (Johnson, 2013). Success at a later stage depends on accomplishments or resolution of the crisis at an earlier stage. Thus, an unresolved developmental crisis can delay, impede, or impact further development. Erikson's eight stages are described below.

53

Stage 1. Infancy: Trust vs. Mistrust (ages birth to 1 year)

The task here is the development of general security and trust in others. This is based on the child's consistent experiences of getting his or her basic needs met such as love, attention, food, physical contact, and warmth. Children whose needs are met by loving, reliable adults are more likely to be optimistic, secure, sociable, and trustful of others. Children whose needs are met by apathetic, inconsistent adults are less likely to develop these traits. At this stage, children need adults who promptly and consistently attend to their needs.

Stage 2. Toddler: Autonomy vs. Shame and Doubt (approximate ages 1 to 3)

At this stage there is a transition from helpless infant to a toddler who is able to exercise some self-control and act independently. This is the "no" stage or the "terrible twos," in which the task is to develop a sense of autonomy. Saying "no" can be a way to establish this autonomy. At this stage, parents should begin to encourage some independence. Children need to explore and try new things; however, they should be given tasks and problems that are within their ability to accomplish. As well, children should be encouraged for both their attempts and successes. Being overly controlling or setting unrealistic expectations can result in shame and doubt and impede development.

Stage 3. Early Childhood: Initiative vs. Guilt (approximate ages 3 to 6)

This stage occurs during the preschool and kindergarten years. At this stage, the task is to initiate activities in order to assert control over the environment. Children do this by planning and directing play, making up games, and by pretending and engaging in make-believe. This is also the stage at which children begin to learn social norms and rules.

Not recognizing the development stage, a mistake sometimes made in kindergarten classrooms is to eliminate play so that children will "learn" more. This ignores the fact that children at this stage learn best through play. For healthy social, emotional, and intellectual development, play should be an important part of preschool and kindergarten classrooms. Learning is greatly enhanced at this stage when it is aligned with play. This means that play should be used as a pedagogical tool in preschool and kindergarten classrooms.

Another mistake is the "push-down curriculum." Here a first-grade curriculum and pedagogical methods are pushed down into a kindergarten classroom. The mistaken assumption here is that by starting earlier, children will be further along in later grades. Since these practices are not developmentally appropriate (NAEYC, 2020), this does not occur.

At this stage, children often imitate adult behaviors. Make-believe and pretending are important here as children explore their environments and come to understand the world. Here, children need opportunities to investigate and manipulate their environment. They also need freedom to experiment and do a lot of "messing around." Finally, they need opportunities to make simple decisions like, *"Would you like oatmeal or cold cereal for breakfast?"* If provided these opportunities, children develop a sense of initiative, and feel secure in making decisions and trying new things. However, children exposed to parents who are overly controlling or highly critical as well as children who do not have sufficient opportunities to initiate activities, explore their environments, experiment, and play may have difficulties with development at the next stage.

Stage 4. Middle Childhood: Industry (or Competence) vs. Inferiority (approximate ages 6 to 11)

At this stage children are trying to build a sense of competence and achievement. The task here is to develop self-worth by learning new skills and successfully creating products or performing skills. For the first time, children are expected to meet the demands of school, peer groups, and parents. They are also compared to a group "norm" for the first time. For healthy social and emotional development, it is important that children experience some success at this stage

Parents and teachers of children in grades one through five should try to help all children find things with which they can be successful (drama, art, citizenship, social skills, sports, hobbies, as well as academic subjects). All children must be allowed to experience success in some way. This does not mean that we should lower standards. Neither does it mean that we should mindlessly "good job" them. Rather, it suggests that we expand experiences, activities, and ways to demonstrating learning.

Specific things parents and teachers can do to help successful development at this stage include the following:

- Present new learning that is within students' zone of proximal development and use scaffolding to ensure success (see Chapter 3).
- Break up more complex tasks into more manageable tasks.
- Arrange learning in small, manageable steps and recognize or reward each step.

- Help students set realistic goals and celebrate their attainment.
- Encourage children to see their own growth instead of comparing themselves to their classmates or a mythical norm.
- De-emphasize competition in sports and other areas.
- Create a varied and differentiated curriculum to meet the diverse needs of all learners.
- Provide support for students who seem discouraged.
- Acknowledge and accept as normal differences in learning and learning rates.
- Reinforce children for taking risks and trying new things.
- Reinforce the idea that failure in some things is normal and expected.

Stage 5. Adolescence: Identity vs. Role Confusion (approximate ages 12 to 18)

This stage represents a period of intense intrapersonal exploration and experimentation. The task here is to achieve a stable sense of identity. (James Marica's description of identity crisis is described below.) Besides physical and psychological changes taking place, adolescents at this stage are dealing with major life questions. They are working to identify their personal values, beliefs, and goals. As well, adolescents are transitioning from childhood to early adulthood and making important decisions related to values, future occupations, relationships, sexuality, gender roles, families, and belief systems. And even though it may be irritating to the adults around them, it is psychologically necessary for adolescents to rebel against authority to some degree. This is one part of developing a sense of identity as they discover, explore, and refine their own values.

Things that parents and teachers can do to help successful development at this stage include the following:

- Encourage students to work out their own values in small-group settings using moral dilemmas and values clarification activities (see Appendix B).
- In small groups, present students with real-life ethical dilemmas that do not have clear answers and then provide them with time to work out their answers.
- Expect and honor students' experimentation with different roles and identities knowing that this will not usually stabilize fully at this stage.
- Be open to students who question cultural norms and values.
- In the classroom, ask open-ended questions for which you do not know the answers.

- Expose students to a variety of subject areas, occupations, career options, ideas, and philosophies.
- Provide students increasingly more opportunities to make choices.

Stage 6. Young Adulthood: Intimacy vs. Isolation (approximate ages 18 to 40)

The primary task at this stage is to develop the ability to maintain intimate personal relationships with others. Establishing a sense of identity at the previous stage is critical for development at this stage. Here one learns to trust, communicate, and live within a variety of types of relationships such as a marriage, partner, and significant other relationship; friendship relationships; or group-alliance relationships.

Some of the tasks here include developing the ability to trust and be trusted, to confide and provide confidence, to be open and accept openness, to be intimate and accept intimacy, and to be honest with oneself and others. Other tasks include learning how to listen, empathize, and communicate within a relationship. Successful completion of this stage can result in happy relationships, as well as a sense of safety, commitment, and care within a relationship. An inability to learn and to develop these skills here can lead to isolation.

Stage 7. Adulthood: Generativity vs. Stagnation (approximate ages 40 to 65)

This stage encompasses middle age, during which the primary task is to develop one's personal and professional life. One seeks to contribute to society or make a mark in ways that will outlast the individual. The individual wants to stand for something or accomplish something. This could include raising children, being productive at work, creating new things, establishing new programs, becoming involved in community activities, being part of service organizations, or making a difference through helping relationships. In some ways, the person sees him or herself as being a significant part of a bigger picture, of doing something that makes a difference. Failure to resolve this task can result in what is known as a midlife crisis. Here people become stagnant and feel unproductive. They may feel disconnect or uninvolved with society.

Stage 8. Old Age: Integrity vs. Despair (approximate ages 65 to death)

The task here is to recognize and adjust to aging and acknowledge the process. Specifically, one seeks to understand and come to grips with one's life.

To do this, one must reflect and review accomplishments as well as failures. Essentially, the following questions are being asked, "Was my life worthwhile? Did I accomplish the goals I set out to accomplish? Did I learn the lessons necessary?"

Successful resolution at this stage is highly dependent on the successful resolution of crises or accomplishing the tasks in last stage. Success here results in ego integrity. Here, one recognizes and embraces all parts of self and acknowledges the prospect of death. Unsuccessful resolution results in despair, in which one might feel that their life has been wasted. A person may experience regrets and be left with feelings of bitterness and despair.

JAMES MARCIA'S THEORY OF ADOLESCENT IDENTITY

As described above, in stage 5 adolescents engage in intense exploration and experimentation on a variety of levels and in different ways. James Marcia extended Erikson's work by focusing on the identity tasks faced by adolescents. He described an identity crisis as a time when adolescents strive to make decisions about possible values, beliefs, future occupations, religious ideas, philosophy and values, belief systems, gender roles, and sex.

The Four Status Points

The four status points related to adolescent identity are *diffused identity, identify foreclosure, moratorium,* and *identity achievement.*

Diffused identity. Here the person has no clear sense of identity. There is little or no commitment to any values or set of beliefs, no decisions about future occupations or long-term goals, and a general lack of direction. This identity status is equated with low self-esteem.

Identity foreclosure. At this identity status point, the person has adopted a sense of values and beliefs; however, this sense of identity has been given to the person, usually by a parent or an institution. In other words, the belief system comes from the outside in. Little processing, self-reflection, or questioning occurs here. The person has foreclosed the possibility of achieving his or her own identity; instead, it is linked with another. This could be a person, family, group, culture, or other influence. This identity status is also equated with low self-esteem.

Moratorium. Here the person is in the process of exploring or trying on a variety of values, beliefs, and career choices. The person is actively engaged in searching for an identity. He or she is undergoing an identity crisis (a good thing) and has chosen not to make a commitment to any sense of identity for the time being. This is a healthy state and is generally associated with high self-esteem.

Identity achievement. After reflecting and fully processing questions related to values and beliefs, the person has a firm sense of who she or he is and wants to be. A commitment has been made to a set of values, beliefs, and possible occupations. Also, the person has embraced gender roles, personal values related to sexuality, and religious beliefs. This is a strong identity status and is equated with a high sense of self-esteem.

Identity Issues Throughout Life

Adolescence is when our struggle for identity is most intense; however, we revisit identity issues at varying levels in different ways throughout our lives. Decisions about who we are and want to be can occur abruptly at transition points, such as a divorce, the death of a spouse, or a change in jobs. It can also occur subtly over time as we embrace new understandings, values, or belief systems. And finally, it can occur with personal development or psychological growth.

Chapter Nine

Moral Development

Lawrence Kohlberg and Carol Gilligan

MORALITY

This chapter describes two theories related to moral development: Lawrence Kohlberg's *levels of moral reasoning* and Carol Gilligan's *stages of the ethics of care*. Both theories have come under criticism in recent years for a variety of reasons. The usual complaint is that the research upon which they were based was not valid or reliable. However, remember that a theory is a way to explain a set of facts. Different theories describe different facts differently. And theories do not predict human behavior; rather, they help us understand human behavior. So it is with these two theories.

Defining Our Terms

We will begin by defining our terms. What is morality? What is a moral person? If you observed a moral person, what behaviors might you see? Is morality the absence of negative traits or presence of positive traits? Can you have both kinds of traits and still be considered to be a moral person? What then is immorality? These are all questions for which there are no easy answers.

   Some might describe morality as a code of behavior based on a set of values. But what values? Whose values are these? Where did they come from? Others might define morality as a matter of conforming to the rules of "right" conduct. Here, moral behaviors would be those that fall within defined boundaries. But who defines the boundaries? What criteria were used? Still others would define morality as adopting and adhering to traditional values. But whose tradition? The tradition of indigenous people? A feminist tradition? An African American tradition? A White, male, Eurocentric tradition?

A corporate tradition? A Latinx tradition? A workers' tradition? A Buddhist tradition?

Defining Morality

A purely behavioral view of morality would describe it as a set of behaviors. But are there any behaviors that can be thought to be universally right and wrong in every situation? Think about this: Long ago there was man living in a small fishing village who went out during the night and sank all the boats in the village. The villagers were outraged at this immoral behavior. It is wrong to destroy the property of others. His actions deprived the villagers of their ability to feed their families. So they beat him and destroyed his house. But it was later learned that the man knew that an attack from an invading army was imminent. The villagers were able to escape the invaders by crossing a bridge and burning it down after them. Sinking the boats gave the villagers enough time to safely flee into the mountains. Had the invading army had access to the boats, hundreds of lives would have been lost. Sinking the villagers' boats was the moral thing to do. The man did it at great cost.

A thought experiment: Think of the most heinous act you can imagine. Image now that space aliens came to you and said that unless you commit such an act, they would blow up the planet. What would be the moral thing to do? This is merely a thought experiment. Nobody is recommending that anybody commit heinous acts or blow up the planet. It simply shows that defining morality strictly in terms of behaviors can be limiting.

This does not mean that everything is relative or that there is no such thing as right and wrong. It does not mean that moral issues should not be addressed in the classroom. Far from it. The classroom is exactly the place to have these discussions (see Appendix B).

The following is a concept of morality that can applied in most classrooms: Morality is any thought, behavior, or action that serves to nurture or give to the self, others, and the environment. Immorality then would be any thought, behavior, or action that takes from or harms the self, other people, or the environment. Often, the most moral response is determined by what is the greatest good for the greatest number. Things are seldom black and white.

KOHLBERG'S LEVELS OF MORAL REASONING

Lawrence Kohlberg's (1984) research was not focused on behaviors, but on the subjects' reasoning behind their behaviors, or their intentions. From this he developed his theory of moral development. This theory describes six stages of moral reasoning at three different levels.

Pre-Conventional Level

The first two stages are described as pre-conventional levels of moral reasoning. Here right and wrong are based primarily on external circumstances (punishments and rewards).

Stage 1: Punishment. At the very lowest stage of moral reasoning, your behavior is guided primarily by the need to avoid punishment. You are motivated to act, not by what is right and good, but rather by what will enable you to avoid some unpleasant condition. Here, morality is under external control. However, when the threat of punishment disappears, the behavior reappears. This is true with rats in a Skinner cage and human beings in a classroom.

Stage 2: Reward. At this stage of moral reasoning, your behavior is determined primarily by what will earn you a reward. You are motivated to act based on what will get you something you desire. Morality here is also under external control. When the external rewards are extinguished, any behaviors that were learned or displayed are extinguished as well.

Analysis and application. This might help us understand the motivation for students' behavior. In the classroom, when a negative behavior is displayed, ask yourself, why is the student doing this? What reward does the student hope to gain here? What punishment or negative consequence is the student trying to avoid? As well, the motivation behind a negative behavior often is not conscious to the individual acting out. As described in Chapter 7, a negative behavior in one place could be a response to a negative experience in another. If children are experiencing trauma or abuse at home, they may display negative behaviors at school.

In terms of using rewards and punishment for behavior management, any plan that is based solely on this will be limited. You may see some short-term changes, but when the external reward or punishment is diminished the behavior eventually returns. This is not to imply that behavioral strategies should not be used in a school, but that they should be used with other things (including a healthy relationship with the teacher and friends).

As an example: Mr. Johnson taught second grade. Tim was one of his students. Tim had a hard time with his behavior in class and frequently got in trouble on the playground. Mr. Johnson put Tim on a contingency contract. He would get a smiley face, straight face, or frowny face on a contract four times a day based on his behavior. At the end of the week, he would take his contract down to the counselor or principal and share. His parents also looked for the contract every Friday. The contract was successful because it helped Tim focus on problem behaviors during the day and it held him accountable. However, the power of the contract was not in the reward but in the relationship. Four times a day, Mr. Johnson would have a short, meaningful interaction with him. And every Friday he could share his success with the counselor or principal. The contingency contract along with the human interaction is what made this approach to behavior management successful.

Conventional Level

The next two stages are at the conventional level. At this level there are internal standards involved in determining right and wrong; however, there is little reflection or personalizing of these standards.

Stage 3: Social approval. This is sometimes called the good-boy/good-girl stage of moral reasoning. At this stage of moral reasoning, your behavior is guided by that which is approved by others or by social conformity. That which is approved by the dominant social group is the final authority on all moral questions. Morality here is still under external control. This stage of moral reasoning is prevalent in middle school and high school when belonging to or being approved by the group is very important. Being part of a group can provide people with a sense of identify, safety, and belonging; however, people are then dependent on the group for the development of a belief system and a sense of right and wrong. Belief systems and moral reasoning at the group level tend to focus more on conformity and allegiance rather than on right or wrong.

Stage 4: The law. Behaviors at this stage of moral reasoning are guided by laws and rules of a society, culture, institution, or religious order. The law or rule is the final say with all moral questions. Since autonomous thought is conceded to the law, morality here is still externally dependent. In its purest form, computers could answer the great moral questions of the day. Behaviors either do or do not fall within certain parameters. One of the dangers of moral reasoning at this stage is that the law can be used to excuse wrongdoing or a lack of response. It can also be used to shed responsibility for evil and destructive behavior: *"We were just following orders."* Of course, what is legal and what is moral are often different things. As an example, segregation based on race was once legal but it was never moral.

Analysis and application. This is called the conventional level for good reason: It is the level at which people tend to operate most of the time. However, nobody operates at any one level exclusively and every human being uses lower levels of moral reasoning at times.

In the classroom, you can help students examine stage 3 moral reasoning (social approval) by presenting models of accomplished people who were not afraid to challenge social rules and norms (Lady Gaga comes to mind). You can also ask students to define their own set of classroom rules. Rules should be stated in the positive (the behavior you want to see), and you should always ask students to explain why the rule is important.

Finally, ask students to develop their own set of standards for ethical be-havior, both in and out of school. This invites them to examine current rules and social norms. In doing these types of activities, the product students come up with is not nearly as important as the process used to discuss norms and values. For example, in high school you might ask students to develop an ethical guide to dating. Having both single-gender groups and mixed-gender groups would expose students to a variety of moral reasoning. It is a Vy-gotskian idea that we develop our reasoning from the outside in. This means that hearing the thoughts and reasoning of others enables us to internalize relevant thought patterns.

Post-Conventional, Autonomous, or Principled Level

This level of moral reasoning is beyond that of conventional moral reasoning. We see the beginning of autonomous thought.

Stage 5: Social contract. At this stage of moral reasoning your behaviors are guided by the preservation of social order. Here, you may disagree with some of the rules and laws, but you know that they are necessary for an or-derly and just society. You understand that rules and laws are created based on what is perceived to be the greatest good for the greatest number of people at a particular time and place. However, situations often change and as such, rules and laws need to evolve. People operating at this stage are willing to adhere to the law in order to preserve social order; however, they are also willing seek change when necessary. And when seeking change, they tend to work within the system.

Stage 6: Universal principles. This is the highest stage of moral reason-ing. Here you realize that truth is the final reality. Right action is determined by your conscience in accordance with a set of universal principles regardless of the consequences. These principles are generally those that accord dignity and worth to all humans, plant life, animal life, and ecosystems. You are will-ing to work within the system, society, or institution but you often find your-self working outside of them to seek necessary changes. People operating at this level are willing to question or challenge the status quo. They confront injustice, moral hypocrisy, double standards, discrimination, and inequity. Very few people operate consistently at this level; however, those who do are often not tolerated by the systems and institutions in which they operate. Martin Luther King Jr., Malcom X., Abraham Lincoln, Gandhi, and Jesus are some examples of people operating at stage 6.

Analysis and application. As irritating as they can sometimes be, people willing to operate at post-conventional levels are necessary for a healthy democracy, society, business, religious organization, school, or classroom.

They are essential for the evolution of society. We are most comfortable with stage 5 behaviors (when they align with our own views). We are a bit less comfortable with people operating at stage 6. These are the trouble-makers, the agents of change. They often are willing to operate outside the system. However, people who are truly operating at this level never resort to violence, destruction, personal attacks, propaganda, control, or domination.

School activities focusing on this level are most developmentally appropriate at the middle and high school level (although they can be adopted for lower levels). Here, students take on real issues to promote real-life change at school or in the community. They include projects aimed at addressing issues such as social justice, systemic racism, poverty, the school-to-prison pipeline, climate change, mental health, LGBTQ rights, disability rights, or other issues.

GILLIGAN'S STAGES OF ETHICAL CARE

Carol Gilligan (1998) contended that Kohlberg's research excluded and devalued women's ways of moral reasoning. His theories on moral development were put forth by a male, in a male-dominant society, using only male subjects, and thus were biased in favor of men. She had a point. Using extensive interviews with girls ages 6 to 18, she postulated that women have differing moral reasoning tendencies than men. According to Gilligan, women tend to think of right and wrong (morality) in terms of caring relationships and connections whereas men tend to think in terms of rules and justice. She argued that these differences were largely a result, not of biological influences, but of social influences and gender conditioning occurring in a context in which women's ways of thinking were often undervalued compared to men's. As society continues to evolve (hopefully), these differences will continue to diminish.

Gilligan described three stages of ethical care:

State I. Pre-conventional morality. The goal here is for individual survival. You look for that which is best for yourself. Right and wrong are determined by what is best for you. For growth to occur, there must be a transition from selfishness to responsibility for others.

Stage II. Conventional morality. At this stage, self-sacrifice is seen as goodness. You learn to care for others and that selfishness is wrong. For growth to occur, there must be a transition from goodness to holistic truth. There is a realization that you too are a person. Caring for others also means caring for yourself. Indeed, you cannot fully nurture and give to others if you do not also nurture and give to yourself.

Stage III. Post-conventional morality. At this stage, you embrace the principles of nonviolence and universal care. You do not hurt others or yourself. You learn that it is just as wrong to ignore your own welfare as it is to ignore the welfare of others. You see the interconnectedness of all things. All of life exists within a system. A system is an interacting and interdependent set of elements working together to form a unified whole. What impacts one small part of the system impacts the whole.

Part II

HUMAN CAPACITY

Chapter Ten

Intelligence

We know that intelligence is important. Most people would rather have more of it than less of it. But what exactly is it? Is it the ability to produce high scores on intelligence tests? Is it the ability to earn good grades? Is it the ability to remember information? Is it the ability to process numbers quickly? Or perhaps it is the ability to learn how to play musical instruments, speak different languages, play different sports, win at poker, solve puzzles, create new inventions, make money, or figure out how to operate computer programs?

Some would define intelligence as an innate cognitive ability. We know that cognition means thinking, so it would be one's inborn ability to think. But what should one think about? How exactly should one think? Is there a particular way of thinking that is better than another?

A PSYCHOMETRIC VIEW OF INTELLIGENCE

This section examines a psychometric view of intelligence.

A Bit of History

The idea of quantifying or describing intelligence numbers started with Alfred Binet back at the turn of the last century. In 1904 he was hired by the French minister of public instruction to help identify children who seemed unable to learn at an average rate in public schools. Once identified, these children were to be sent to alternative schools where they would receive special help appropriate to their needs. Binet had to find a way to determine which students were within the normal range of intellectual functioning and which were below the normal range. He came up with a test that was to measure intelligence: the intelligence quotient test or IQ test.

The IQ Score

In 1916, Stanford psychologist Lewis Terman refined Alfred Binet's original intelligence test. His work is the basis for today's Stanford-Binet Intelligence Scale. This test was used to compare people of the same age or category across a normal distribution. If the distribution of scores represents a normal population, the test scores (or any other kinds of scores) would look like the bell-shaped pattern in Figure 10.1. (The horizontal axis represents students' test scores going from lowest to highest; the vertical axis represents the percentage of students who obtained each score.) It is normal (hence a normal distribution), to have a whole bunch of students at the average range. It is also normal to have very few students at the very high end and very few students at the very low end. Half of all the scores are above average and half are below average. That is what average is. IQ scores of 85–115 are considered to be within the average range. Sixty-eight percent of the population falls within this range.

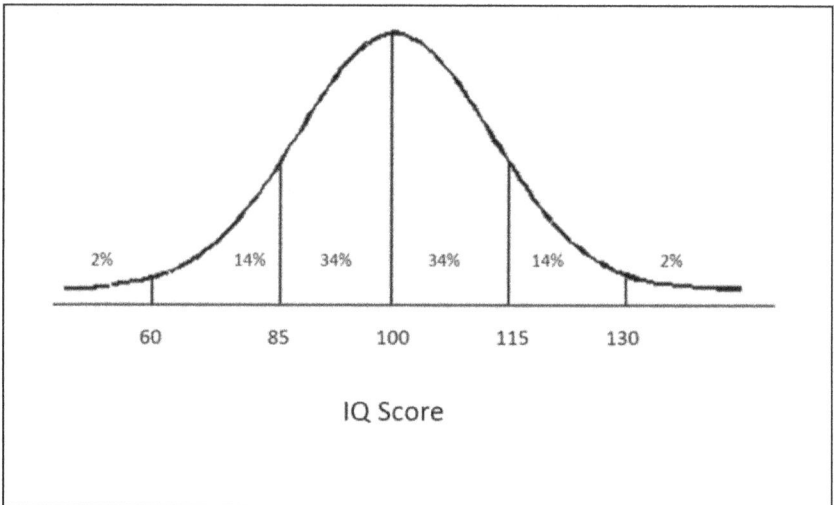

Figure 10.1. Bell-shaped curve for a normal distribution of scores.

Fallacy of Numbers

According to the psychometric view above, intelligence is what is measured on tests. While it is comforting to have a precise description of intelligence like this, attaching a number to something does not make it any more real. Robert Sternberg (1996) describes four problems associated with IQ tests:

1. They represent a very narrow range of thinking. Who decided what types of problems were to be on these intelligence tests? Who determined which type of thinking was important? The problems found on these tests tend to rely on only logical-deductive or analytic thinking. As well, they do not represent the variety of types of thinking that are used in real-life situations to solve problems or create products and performances.

2. They are highly dependent on vocabulary and exposure to concepts. You could have a high-functioning brain, but if, because of environmental situations, you have not been exposed to certain words, concepts, or thinking strategies, your ability to score well is greatly diminished even though your low score would have nothing to do with your ability to think.

3. They have little predictive value. The biggest predictor of these tests is your ability to do equally well on a similar test. There may be some correlation with school grades or school-based performance, but there is little correlation with success in the real world.

4. They do not measure creative or practical thinking abilities. The ability to generate ideas and to apply ideas in the real world are every bit as important in achieving most types of success as the type of thinking measured on these tests.

DEFINING INTELLIGENCE

Not all theories of intelligence fit into the comfortable, linear conception of intelligence as measured by the Stanford-Binet Intelligence Scale. Two of these theories are described here.

Charles Spearman's Two-Factor Theory of Intelligence

Charles Spearman (1863–1945) was a British psychologist who took a psychometric view of intelligence but proposed a "two-factor" theory of intelligence. According to him, there were two factors that made up intelligence: The first factor was called "g" or general intelligence. This can be thought of as your brain's general processing capabilities, a type of intelligence that could be applied to many types of tasks. Using a computer analogy, this would be the amount of memory that can be used to process a variety of different tasks. If you have more of it (memory), you can process many things quickly. The second factor was called "s" or specific intelligence, which were the types of intelligence involved in specific tasks such as math, writing, or vocabulary activities.

Fluid and Crystallized Theory Intelligence

John Horn and Raymond Cattell (1966) described two types of intelligence called fluid and crystallized intelligence. Fluid intelligence is somewhat related to Spearman's concept of "g." It is the brain's general processing power or the ability to process, apply, and manipulate data (both internal and external), as well as the ability to adapt to circumstances and recognize patterns.

According to their theory, fluid intelligence tends to decrease slightly with age. Crystallized intelligence is one's accumulated knowledge. This includes declarative knowledge such as vocabulary; basic information and concepts; and also procedural knowledge such as processes, thinking skills, pattern recognition, and problem-solving strategies. This type of intelligence tends to increase with age. Thus, any decrease in fluid intelligence is offset by increases in crystallized intelligence. This points to the importance of continued reading, studying, learning, cognitive activities, games, and other mental exercises in order to maintain one's intellectual capacities into old age.

DEFINING INTELLIGENCE: EXPANDED VIEWS

This section presents theories of intelligence that describe people not as more intelligent or less intelligent; rather, they present people as intelligent in different ways. For example, the type of intelligence necessary to be an effective teacher in a first-grade classroom is much different than that of a scientist working on a complex research project at a university. The type of intelligence valued and displayed by Sue Bird on a basketball court is different than that of J. K. Rowling writing books, Jerry Seinfeld creating comedy, or Miles Davis playing a blues solo on his trumpet. Each domain values different traits and each utilizes a different type of thinking to achieve mastery.

Gardner's Theory of Multiple Intelligences

Howard Gardner's book *Frames of Mind* (1993) was instrumental in getting schools to start thinking about intelligence in much broader terms. He defined intelligence as the ability to solve problems or create products that are valued within a cultural setting. Instead of a single entity with many facets, Gardner identified eight different kinds of intelligence (Checkley, 1997):

1. Linguistic intelligence is the ability to use words to describe or communicate ideas. Examples of people who use this intelligence are poets, writers, storytellers, comedians, public speakers, public relations experts, politicians, journalists, editors, and professors.

2. Logical-mathematical intelligence is the ability to perceive patterns in numbers or reasoning, to use numbers effectively, or to reason well. Examples—mathematician, scientist, computer programmer, statistician, logician, or detective.

3. Spatial intelligence is the ability to perceive the visual-spatial world accurately (and not get lost) and to transform it. Examples—hunter, scout, guide, interior decorator, architect, artist, or sculptor.

4. Bodily-kinesthetic intelligence is expertise in using one's body. Examples—athlete, mime, or dancer.

5. Musical intelligence is the ability to recognize and produce rhythm, pitch, and timber; to express musical forms; and to use music to express an idea. Examples—composer, director, performer, or musical technician.

6. Interpersonal intelligence is the ability to perceive and appropriately respond to the moods, temperaments, motivations, and needs of other people. Examples—pastor, counselor, administrator, teacher, manager, coach, co-worker, or parent.

7. Intrapersonal intelligence is the ability to access one's inner life, to discriminate between one's emotions, intuitions, and perceptions, and to know one's strengths and limitations. Examples—religious leader, counselor, psychotherapist, writer, or philosopher.

8. Naturalistic intelligence is the ability to recognize and classify living things (plants, animals) as well as sensitivity to other features of the natural world (rocks, clouds). Examples—naturalist, hunter, scout, farmer, or environmentalist.

So how is a teacher to use Gardner's theory? Two ideas: First, let students know that there are different ways to be smart and that it is okay to be good at some things and not good at others. Everybody is good at something and nobody is good at everything. Many classroom teachers put up posters describing each of these types of intelligence. Some even expand on this by asking students to think of other ways to be smart and then let them create additional posters.

Second, in your future classroom, design learning experiences, activities, and assignments that use these different ways of thinking. Try to incorporate the varied types of intelligence into your lessons and units (this is not always possible). By using these different ways of thinking to manipulate subject matter content, students will see things from a broader perspective, learn more, and learn more deeply (Diaz-Lefebvre, 2006; Kornhaber, 2004).

Existential Intelligence

Gardner has considered a ninth intelligence: existential intelligence (1999). This would be a trait concerned with issues regarding the nature of existence and ultimate issues. Others have explored this area. Sisk and Torrance (2001) use the term "spiritual intelligence" to denote the ability to use multisensory approaches to problem-solving and the ability to listen to your inner voice. Zohar and Marshall (2001) describe it as

> the intelligence with which we address and solve problems of meaning and value, the intelligence with which we can place our actions and lives in a wider, richer, meaning-giving context, the intelligence with which we can assess that one course of action or one life-path is more meaningful than another. (pp. 3–4)

Vaughan (2003) portrays spiritual intelligence as a different way of knowing, a part of self that is concerned with the life of the mind and spirit and its relationship to being in the world. For the purpose of this book, spiritual intelligence will be defined as the ability to become attuned to and utilize multiple dimensions of self, and to perceive and experience the seamless connection between self, others, and the universe.

Spiritual intelligence is a concept you are not likely to encounter in any formal way in public school settings. So why include it here? There are dimensions of the human experience that cannot be measured or quantified yet still play a prominent role in helping many people solve problems, make decisions, and come to know the world. Thus, a study of humans and human learning should take into account all dimensions of the human experience.

Sternberg's Triarchic Theory of Intelligence

Robert Sternberg (1985) defines intelligence as the ability to adapt to and shape one's environment to meet one's needs or purposes. His triarchic theory of intelligence (Sternberg & Williams, 2002) describes three types of thinking that are used together to meet this end:

Creative or generative thinking. You are able to generate many ideas, synthesize two or more ideas, create original ideas, think outside the box, find ideas that nobody else has considered, or utilize divergent thinking and inductive reasoning.

Analytical or evaluative thinking. You are able to evaluate ideas, analyze ideas, organize ideas, compare ideas, or utilize convergent thinking and deductive reasoning.

Pragmatic thinking. You are able to implement, apply, or adapt the ideas produced through generative and evaluative thinking to meet the demands of your particular situation.

According to Sternberg's theory, intelligence can be found in any domain. For example, intelligence related to teaching would include the ability to use all three of these types of thinking to create effective learning experiences. An intelligent teacher would be able to (a) generate ideas for creating new learning experiences and solving problems related to teaching and learning, (b) evaluate and organize those ideas, and then (c) adapt and apply them to his or her particular setting.

Another example of this can be found in some of the popular survival shows on TV in which people are dropped into a wilderness environment and have to survive for a given amount of time. Here they must (a) generate ideas for building shelters and getting food, (b) evaluate the ideas for effectiveness, and then (c) make them work. It is a fascinating display of these types of thinking applied within a survival setting.

This view of intelligence describes three broad thinking processes that can then be applied to any areas. Sternberg (1996) also supports the idea that intelligence is not a fixed entity. That is, it is something that can be improved by teaching problem-solving strategies, thinking skills, and other types of cognitive strategies.

Successful Intelligence

Sternberg also describes what he calls successful intelligence, which he defines as "an integrated set of abilities used to attain success in life, however a person chooses to define success or however it might be defined within a particular sociocultural context" (Sternberg & Grigorenka, 2000, p. 6). Depending on what you value or what your culture values, success might include one or more of kinds of accomplishments listed in Textbox 10.1.

TEXTBOX 10.1. DIFFERENT TYPES OF ACCOMPLISHMENTS

- Healthy relationships and family life
- Creative artistic freedom and expression
- Happiness, peace of mind
- An accumulation of wealth or material possessions
- Accomplishments: athletic, artistic, scholarly, business, political, scientific, etc.
- Power and importance
- Fame and prestige
- Honor, integrity, and truthfulness
- The ability to give to and nurture
- Free time, freedom, and a lack of responsibilities
- Developing or running a successful business or some other type of enterprise

- Wisdom
- Wholeness, spiritual gifts
- Leadership roles

Sternberg (2003) describes three characteristics shared by successfully intelligent people:

1. **Successfully intelligent people recognize their strengths and use them to compensate for their weaknesses.** Students are described in terms of what they cannot do. Their weaknesses are identified and overemphasized in an attempt to remediate them. Instead, time would be better spent teaching students how to use their strengths to compensate for or correct weaknesses.
2. **Successfully intelligent people are able to adapt to, shape, and select their environments.** To illustrate, Polly moved in with Samantha. She soon found out that Samantha was messier than she had imagined. One trait in particular that bothered Polly was the fact that Samantha always left dirty dishes in the sink. To adapt to her environment, Polly could tell herself that it really did not matter. She might also start eating most of her meals outside the apartment. To shape her environment she could talk with Samantha. She could create a chart and assign dishwashing days. Or she could hide every dish except one pot and pan, and two plates, dishes, cups, and sets of silverware. To select a new environment Polly could try to get out of her lease or look for a less messy roommate to trade places with.
3. **Successfully intelligent people are able to use analytical, creative, and practical thinking to create products or performances, to solve problems, or to achieve their goals.** To illustrate this idea, look at the two examples described above under "Sternberg's Triarchic Theory of Intelligence."

We must never lose sight of the fact that what really matters most in the world is not inert intelligence but successful intelligence: that balanced combination of analytical, creative, and practical thinking skills. Successful intelligence is not an accident; it can be nurtured and developed in our schools by providing students, even at an early age, with curricula that will challenge their creative and practical intelligence, not only their analytic skills (Sternberg & Grigorenka, 2000, p. 269).

Goleman's Theory of Emotional Intelligence

The last type of intelligence considered here is emotional intelligence (EI). This is a type of social intelligence somewhat related to Gardner's conception of intrapersonal and interpersonal intelligence above. It is the ability to perceive and understand emotions, manage one's emotion, monitor one's own and others' emotions, and to use that information to guide one's thinking and actions (Goleman, 1995; Pfeiffer, 2000). Emotional intelligence involves abilities that can be categorized into five domains (see Textbox 10.2).

TEXTBOX 10.2. EMOTIONAL INTELLIGENCE

- **Self-awareness:** Observing yourself and recognizing a feeling as it happens (intrapersonal intelligence)
- **Managing emotions:** Handling feelings so that they are appropriate; understanding the origin of emotions; finding ways to handle negative emotions (fears, anxieties, anger, and sadness)
- **Motivating oneself:** Channeling emotions in the service of a goal; ability to delay gratification and stifle impulses to obtain a greater goal
- **Empathy:** Sensitivity to others' feelings and concerns and taking their perspectives; ability to appreciate the differences in how people feel about things
- **Handling relationships:** Managing emotions in others; social competence and social skills

The five domains described in Textbox 10.2 can all be addressed within a general education curriculum. For example, we can teach students to identify and become more aware of their own emotions and inner worlds (self-awareness). We can teach them to manage their emotions by helping them discover healthy responses to their feelings of anger, anxiety, sadness, or other emotions. We can help students define goals for themselves and describe the steps necessary to achieve those goals. And we can also help students develop empathy and learn how to handle a variety of types of relationships. It is very appropriate then that these elements be included in our curricula, not as separate curriculum items, but rather as embedded into social studies, health, literature, and other curriculum areas.

CONCLUDING THOUGHTS

Intelligence is certainly much more than a little number. However, after all that has been written on multiple views of intelligence in the past, most schools still rely solely on quantitative data from standardized achievement or ability tests to define both intelligence and achievement. This practice fails in helping to develop the potentials of those students whose talents and ways of thinking fall outside the narrow definitions imposed upon them by schools.

Chapter Eleven

Creativity

Creativity is a trait that has helped to produce some of the most important innovations in human history. It has enabled us to solve some of our most complex and compelling problems. The word "creativity" is even included in most definitions of giftedness used for gifted and talented programs in schools.

> Students capable of high performance include those with demonstrated achievement or potential ability in one or more of these areas: general intellectual, specific academic subjects, *creativity*, leadership, and visual/performing arts. (Minnesota Department of Education, 2021)

Clearly creativity is a valuable human trait and yet, it is given little attention in our schools. Why is that? Textbox 11.1. contains a thought experiment.

TEXTBOX 11.1. A THOUGHT EXPERIMENT

A thought experiment: What if creativity were suddenly given the same status as intelligence in our schools?

- Would there be pull-out programs to address the creative needs of highly creative students?
- Would psychometric tests be designed to identify those with creative disabilities?
- Would schools develop programs to remediate the needs of the students who had creative disabilities?
- Would students be given labels to designate their lack of creativity?

- Would there be special rooms for students who had diminished creative capacities?
- Would the word "creativity" start to be found on students' IEPs (individualized education programs)?

UNDERSTANDING CREATIVITY

Creativity is a type of thinking that enables people to generate ideas, invent new ideas, improve old ideas, and recombine existing ideas in a novel fashion (Gallagher & Gallagher, 1994). It is the process of bringing something new into being (May, 1975). Behaviorally, creativity can be defined as the ability to produce work that is novel, high in quality, and appropriate (Feldman et al., 1994; Sternberg & Lubart, 1999). Novel here means that the work is original or unique, something nobody has thought of or done before. Appropriate in this context means that the work is of some aesthetic or pragmatic value (Starko, 2005; Swartz & Perkins, 1990). Torrance describes creativity as

> the process of sensing difficulties, problems, gaps in information, missing elements, something askew; making guesses and formulating hypotheses about these deficiencies; evaluating and testing these guesses and hypotheses; possibly revising and retesting them; and last, communicating the results. (1993, p. 233)

Creativity as Problem-Solving

Creativity is essentially a type of problem-solving (Gardner, 1994). Problems can be found in all domains including the arts, business, science, politics, economics, the military, and even education. Examples of problems include the following: How can we design a car to run on electricity? How can this emotion or idea be expressed through movement, dance, music, or visual art? What kind of a play will enable our team to score a touchdown? How can I make this relationship work? How can this concept be explained so that people understand it? How can this skill be taught? How can I keep my seventh-hour social studies class actively engaged? How can I write a book so that undergraduates can easily understand important concepts related to educational psychology? These are all problems that require some form of creative thinking for their ultimate solution.

Creativity as problem-solving sounds remarkably similar to Gardner's and Sternberg's descriptions of intelligence (see Chapter 10). Indeed, the line between intelligence and creativity becomes blurred when one recognizes that both cognitive traits have equal importance in solving problems and creating products (Sternberg & Lubart, 1991). Creative thinking enhances problem-solving because the ability to generate a lot of ideas and a wide variety of ideas provides a greater range of alternatives to evaluate.

Let us define our terms here: A problem is a difference between the current state and the ideal state (see Chapter 15). However, if you are not aware of a problem in the first place you will have a difficult time solving it. Thus, being able to perceive problems is an important part of creativity (Csikszentmihalyi, 1994). Put another way, creative individuals are able to perceive the difference between what is and what could be.

Redefining Problems

Another trait that enables highly creative people to solve problems is their ability to look at them in different ways (Lipshitze & Waingortin, 1995; Sternberg & Williams, 2002). This is called redefining the problem (Sternberg & Grigorenka, 2000). Effective problem solvers are able to let go of the old ways of thinking, which in turn enables them to generate a variety of novel solutions. This is the "thinking outside the box" cliché with which most are familiar. By freeing themselves from conventional ways of thinking and by examining problems from a variety of angles, highly creative people open themselves up to a variety of new possibilities. Textbox 11.2 contains two examples of problems that have been redefined.

TEXTBOX 11.2. EXAMPLES OF REDEFINING PROBLEMS

- **The problem:** Many new teachers are faced with the problem of classroom management. One way that is often used to define the problem is this: How can I control these students? Solutions often include getting tough, offering rewards, or looking for gimmicks or programs.
  - **The problem redefined:** How can I create learning experiences that provide structure instead of control, and encourage students to learn in ways that are natural to them?
- **The problem:** Oftentimes teachers and parents look for ways to motivate students to read. The problem is typically defined like so: What can I do to get students to read this book or this chapter?
  - **The problem redefined:** How can I find material that students want to read?

Other Traits Associated with Creativity and Highly Creative People

In a 30-year longitudinal study Torrance (1992) found that highly creative and successful people have the following characteristics: delight in deep thinking, tolerance of mistakes, love of one's work, clear purpose, feeling comfortable being a minority of one, and feeling comfortable being different. Other personal traits associated with creativity, creative thinking, and creative people include the following:

- Self-confidence, independence, risk-taking, energy and enthusiasm, adventurousness, curiosity, playfulness, humor, idealism, reflection, sensitivity to problems, ability to define problems, ability to resist premature closure, visualization, analogical thinking, intuition, concentration, nonconformity, unconventionality, and logical thinking (Davis & Rimm, 1998).
- Tolerance for ambiguity, willingness to surmount obstacles, intrinsic motivation, moderate risk-taking, desire for recognition, and willingness to work for recognition (Lynch & Harris, 2001).
- Boldness, courage, freedom, spontaneity, perspicuity, integration, self-acceptance, ability to embrace paradox, ability to put order to chaos, and playfulness (Maslow, 1968).

Creative Thinking

Think for a minute about the types of thinking specifically used in the creative process. What qualities of thought produce work that is novel, high in quality, and appropriate? Torrance (1992) identified four: fluency, flexibility, elaboration, and originality

- **Fluency** is the ability to generate a great many ideas. This type of thinking can be used when looking for possible solutions to problems. This is often known as brainstorming (see Textbox 11.3). It is important with this type of thinking to not evaluate ideas initially. Evaluating ideas comes only after a great number have been generated.
- **Flexibility** is the ability to generate a variety of different ideas or to produce a number of different approaches. For example, what are some other ways we might be able to get a telescope into space? What are some other ways in which we could generate power for our cars and homes? What are some other ways I might learn this material and pass the midterm exam?
- **Elaboration** is the ability to examine the original thing and generate ideas that can be used to make the original thing better, more interesting, more detailed, more complex, or more refined. For example, what could I add to a bike, birthday party, or bathtub to make it better?

- **Originality** is the ability to design or create things that are totally new, unique, or novel; things never before imagined. What are some new types of transportation that we have not yet considered? How else might we prepare preservice teachers to meet the demands of the classroom? How could this theme be expressed in a movie in a way that is unique, novel, and interesting?

The Torrance Test of Creative Thinking (TTCT) (Torrance, 1999), a commonly used creativity test, is designed to measure these four types of thinking. But can creativity really be measured? The jury is still out on this one. While the ability to predict creative achievement is questioned; the TTCT may predict creative potential (Corpley, 2000).

TEXTBOX 11.3. TIPS FOR BRAINSTORMING

Students (and adults), do not naturally know how to brainstorm; thus, they must be taught the process. Initially, this process should be modeled in a large group with the teacher writing down the ideas generated by the class. Later, students can move into small groups. Idea generation works best in pairs or small groups, as students are able to hear a number of ideas. These initial ideas, in turn, serve to generate more ideas. There are four rules for brainstorming. Put these rules in poster form to assist your initial instruction, and then use this poster for quick review when needed:

1. *All ideas must be accepted*. No criticizing or evaluation is allowed. At this stage, bad ideas are just as important as good ideas.
2. *Freewheeling is celebrated*. Creative, bizarre, unusual, and silly ideas are welcomed along with smart-aleck comments and random associations. All of these can be used to stretch our thinking and get us thinking more broadly.
3. *The goal of brainstorming is quantity*. The more ideas we have, the greater our choice is in finding a solution.
4. *Hitchhiking is welcome*. Hitchhiking is when you add to an idea that has already been stated or combine two or more ideas. This is a technique many creative problem solvers use. Encourage your students to do this as well.

Knowledge, Intelligence, and Creativity

To be creative you must first have a body of knowledge (Feldhusen, 1995; Gallagher & Gallagher, 1994; Gardner, 1994; Piirto, 1994). Creativity involves the manipulation of ideas from a knowledge base. Without a body of knowledge there is nothing to manipulate. In other words, without a box there is not a box to step outside of. This is one of the reasons why it is important to have well-structured curricula that lay out plans for presenting students with a fair amount of knowledge in an organized fashion. Among other things, a body of knowledge enhances students' ability to think creatively and to solve problems (Chi et al., 1981; de Groot, 1965).

There is also some relationship between creativity and intelligence (Good & Brophy, 1995). Intelligence is used to facilitate the development of a well-organized knowledge base, thus making it easier to retrieve ideas, relate new information to existing schemas, and manipulate ideas in new and interesting ways (Feldhusen, 1995). However, while some amount of intelligence is required for creative achievement, highly intelligent people are not necessarily highly creative (Starko, 2005). And as pointed out earlier, the line between creativity and intelligence can become blurred as both are instrumental in solving problems.

The Creative Process

The last area examined here is the creative process. Creativity rarely happens by accident. It does not just occur; rather, it is a purposeful act requiring preparation, hard work, and discipline (Marzano et al., 1988). The sudden creative insight that inventors and artists sometimes describe is usually the last step in a long thinking process that occurs over time. Creativity is not a drive through experience. It is not an event, but a process. We can enhance our creativity by attending to the process. The Wallas Model of Creativity (Wallas, 1926), a common model of creativity, proposes four stages of the creative process:

1. **Preparation.** This is the stage at which the problem is first perceived and defined, information about the problem is gathered, and ideas are generated. As examples, we will look at two college students, Polly and Pat, who both attend Mooseville State University. Polly, an English creative writing major, is assigned to write a piece of fiction for her creative writing course. During the preparation stage she has a sense of her topic and she starts brainstorming or listing ideas, and gets background information to help her with her story. Pat, a sociology major, is looking for a research project for his senior paper. During this stage he selects his topic and begins to review the literature and takes notes. Both Polly and Pat have a sense of where they are going at this stage, but it is still unclear what the final product is going to look like.

2. **Incubation.** Here, both the conscious and unconscious mind manipulate the problem and think about possible solutions. New information is related to existing information and existing schemata are reorganized to accommodate new information. Sometimes stages one and two merge into each

other slightly. At this stage Polly is creating outlines and initial drafts. Pat also is creating outlines and initial drafts, but for both, the path they will take is still unclear. Their writing may seem labored at this point. A lot of work at the incubation stage takes place unconsciously. Polly and Pat, who are both good students, know the importance of starting their projects early. This gives them lots of time to process information and to think about their projects with the conscious part of their minds.

3. Illumination. At this stage, the creator suddenly sees the idea, concept, or solution to the problem. Polly and Pat have been preparing, processing, incubating, and percolating. At some point they get a sudden insight about exactly how their story and research project should go. Their projects appear to fall together instantly. Their writing and researching seems almost effortless. However, this "aha" moment would not have occurred had they not prepared, processed, incubated, and percolated.

4. Verification. This is an evaluative stage at which the creator verifies or tests the idea, concept, or solution. At this stage, Polly and Pat have finished their initial drafts and are in the process of revising and getting feedback on their projects. During this stage there may also be a series of little illuminations where the "aha" moment occurs in varying degrees and dimensions. And of course, the ultimate verification is the grade of A they received on their projects and the recognition they received from Mooseville State University for their outstanding creative and scholarly achievements.

Their grade of A also verifies the creative process. A bit of advice for students: It *always* pays to start your assignments and projects early. Some students claim that they work better under the pressure of a deadline at the last minute. While this may strengthen their motivation, it does not result in a better product or performance. By starting early, you will find that you will spend less time and end up with a better product than by starting at the last minute.

Chapter Twelve

Intuition

Along with creativity, intuition has also been an important element in some of humankind's most outstanding innovations and breakthroughs. If our goal is to enable all students (and teachers) to reach their full potential, it would seem to make sense then that we might address this element of human capacity.

WHAT INTUITION MIGHT BE

Intuition is a cognitive function, something our brains do naturally (whether we are aware of it or not), but it is also a mental operation that can be taught directly and deliberately applied. It is a type of thinking that is nonlinear. As well, intuition is a level of awareness or state of consciousness. Nel Noddings defines intuition as "that function that contacts objects directly in phenomena. This direct contact yields something we might call 'knowledge' in that it guides our actions and is precipitated by our own quest for meaning" (Noddings & Shore, 1984, p. 57). Jerome Bruner (1977) defined intuition as "the act of grasping the meaning, significance, or structure of a problem or situation without explicit reliance on the analytic apparatus of one's craft" (p. 60).

Intuition is defined here as a sudden knowing apart from logic or knowledge. It is the ability to make the leap from the known or predictable to something totally different or to realign known information or see facts in totally new ways.

Traditionally, our schools and Western culture have valued logic and reason and devalued intuition and emotion (Miller, 2001). Intuition (and emotion), have been seen as weaknesses in the problem-solving and decision-making process ("*It was just an emotional decision*"). However, it is not an either/or proposition. Intuition and emotion can enhance rational knowing. The same brain that thinks and stores knowledge also emotes and intuits. So of course, we can use both to enhance both thinking and knowing.

Three Levels of Intuition

There are three levels or types of intuition: rational intuition, predictive intuition, and transformational intuition.

- **Rational intuition** is thinking that realigns known information. It is that "aha" experience during which you suddenly see the solution to a problem or get new insight. Often new information is combined with forgotten information to connect the dots in a different way. This type of awareness seems to come when you are sleeping or when your mind is relaxed or thinking of other things. This demonstrates the importance of moving away from the logical mind.
- **Predictive intuition** is thinking that utilizes known information to form new patterns, ideas, or plans. Here you use information to create a hunch, guess, or hypothesis. You are able to perceive the whole based on only partial information. Again, this is something the brain naturally does. Your brain naturally uses partial data to complete the whole picture. For example, your brain organizes the two lines in Figure 12.1 into either a chalice or two people kissing. In Figure 12.2, even though there are no lines to indicate it, your brain naturally creates the picture of a sphere based on partial information.

Figure 12.1. Two lines.

Figure 12.2. Creating a sphere based on partial information.

Predictive intuition is also the type of thinking Jerome Bruner (1977) saw as an important part of inductive reasoning (see Chapter 14). Here students examine many specific examples in order to formulate a general principle. Bruner described intuitive thinking as essential in formulating hypotheses used in the scientific model.

- **Transformational intuition** is thinking or awareness that uses a different kind of sensing to pick up information. This defies most traditional scientific explanations. Here information seems to come from a source outside the individual. This can also be the type of B-cognition described by Abraham Maslow that often occurs when we are working or performing at our highest states during peak experiences (Maslow, 1971).

The Intuitive Process

Intuition can be helpful in knowing and understanding our environments as well as problem-solving and decision-making in the classroom. Master teachers are often able to use their intuition to understand students and situations as well as to identify solutions or make good decisions. Toward this end, Textbox 12.1 has a list of things that can be used to enhance your intuition.

TEXTBOX 12.1 THINGS THAT ENHANCE YOUR INTUITION

1. **Quiet the mind.** Use any technique to get away from the chatter and clutter of your conscious mind. Techniques may include walking, deep breathing, mediation, or relaxation techniques.
2. **Focused attention.** Sustained focused attention with a relaxed mind enables images to bubble up from the unconscious.
3. **Receptive attitude.** You must be in a state in which you are willing and able to open your mind to a variety of thoughts.
4. **Validate images and impressions**. Validate the various images and ideas that come to you when you are using your intuitive process. Everything means something. Even seemingly crazy ideas often lead to useful and creative turns.
5. **Free write.** A free write is where you write down the first word or thought that pops into your mind. The goal is to do it quickly without thinking. This enables you to get around the logical mind and allow the unconscious mind to speak to you.

Problem-Solving and Decision-Making

In Western society, and by extension our schools, there is a tendency to value and use only knowledge and logic to solve problems and make decisions. These two elements are certainly necessary, but they are not sufficient in making balanced decisions. In both your personal and professional life well-balanced decision-making and problem-solving uses four ways of knowing (see Figure 12.3):

Emotion What feelings does it generate?	*Knowledge* What knowledge do you have?
Logic What can you logically deduce or infer from the data?	*Intuition* What does your gut feeling tell you?

Figure 12.3.   Four ways of knowing.

- **Logic.** Logic is used to determine the possible effect of various alternatives and to evaluate the various solutions. Logic is also used to evaluate emotional and intuitive reactions.
- **Knowledge.** Knowledge of similar situations as well as past strategies and solutions that are stored in long-term memory are retrieved. These are compared to the current situation in order to identify effective solutions.

Knowledge can be used to put our emotional reactions and intuitive feelings in context.

- **Intuition.** Intuition can be used to connect the dots, to view knowledge in new ways, or to generate new ideas or identify solutions. It can also be used to test the appropriateness of ideas. What does your gut feeling tell you?
- **Emotion.** Emotions can be used to evaluate the appropriateness of logic and knowledge-based decisions. What does your emotional state tell you about each alternative? What decision feels the best? What feelings or other associations come to mind when you think of each decision?

Chapter Thirteen

Emotions

UNDERSTANDING EMOTIONS

What are these things called emotions?

Mood, Affect, and Temperament

At their core, *emotions* are a physiological response to stimuli that enable humans to react to events of biological or individual significance (LeDoux, 2002). From an evolutionary perspective, these physiological responses promoted survival behavior of the individual or the group. Emotions are short lived, usually lasting only for about 15 seconds. They can survive longer than that if we cultivate them—that is, if we dwell upon them. Think about this again from an evolutionary perspective: Emotions are a response to external stimuli. Emotions lasting too long would impact perception and put us at risk for other external events.

Moods are emotional states that endure longer (Purves et. al, 2008). With moods there is often choice involved. We choose the thoughts upon which we dwell. We get to determine the movie that plays in our head. There is a saying, "Beware of the second arrow." The first arrow is when a negative or hurtful incident occurs and a negative emotion arises. The second arrow is the negative emotion that arises every time you think about the incident. For example, if somebody insults you, you feel badly. Every time you think about that incident you are insulted again and feel badly again. If you keep thinking about it, you will keep being insulted and keep feeling badly. You cannot choose what you feel; however, you can choose what you think about.

Affect is the term used to refer to the outward expression of emotions. It is how your emotions are displayed. *Temperament* is a predisposition to think, respond, and interpret events in certain ways. For example, you can have a grumpy temperament, a happy temperament, a fiery temperament, or easygoing temperament. Temperament is part of one's personality and is a product of one's experience and genetic factors.

Emotional Disorders

In educational settings, emotions are sometimes believed to be out of order. The emotional/behavioral disorder (E/BD) label is given to these students (see Textbox 13.1). They are then put into the special education system. However, once in the system, the focus is rarely on the emotion. It is almost always on the behavior. Here, unwanted behaviors are identified and special plans are written up. These special plans are called Positive Behavior Interventions and Supports or PBIS. PBIS is a behavioral approach for addressing behaviors (but not emotions). Here, "research-based" strategies are implemented with fidelity to make unwanted behaviors go away and desired behaviors appear. Fidelity means that the "research-based" strategies are uniformly applied to all students in exactly the same way regardless of students' particular needs or circumstances. Rewards are then given for the desired behaviors and data are collected.

TEXTBOX 13.1. U.S. DEPARTMENT OF EDUCATION DEFINITION OF EMOTIONAL OR BEHAVIORAL DISORDERS

Emotional or behavioral disorders are defined as an established pattern of one or more of the following emotional or behavioral responses: (a) withdrawal or anxiety, depression, problems with mood, or feelings of self worth; (b) disordered thought processes with unusual behavior patterns and atypical communication styles; or (c) aggression, hyperactivity, or impulsivity.

The established pattern of emotional or behavioral responses must adversely affect educational or developmental performance, including intrapersonal, academic, vocational, or social skills; be significantly different from appropriate age, cultural, or ethnic norms; and be more than temporary, expected responses to stressful events in the environment. The emotional or behavioral responses must be consistently exhibited in at least three different settings, two of which must be educational settings, and one other setting in either the home, childcare, or community. The responses must not be primarily the result of intellectual, sensory, or acute or chronic physical health conditions.

Of course, one of the problems with this approach is that the focus is on the behavior, and not on the emotions behind the behavior. This is not to say that PBIS is not effective in some cases. It is. It provides a scaffold to enable some students to focus on appropriate behaviors. But it is simply one tool among many. It is not the only tool to use. And it is not the best tool to use in all situations. When it is used, it should always be flexibly applied (not used with fidelity) to best meet the needs of each student.

Educational Disorders

As will be described in Chapter 19, often times the E/BD label is given to children who are suffering from trauma, stress, neglect, abuse, or worse. In these cases, their negative behaviors may be a very appropriate response to a negative situation. The E/BD label is also sometimes given to children with a mental health disorder. So now the student has two problems: the initial problem that caused the negative behaviors and then the stigma of having a special education label attached to him or her.

Students who are given an E/BD label often have another label: learning disability (LD). However, if a student is continually frustrated and humiliated by an inability to learn, that student is going to be more apt to display negative behaviors. Again, negative behavior is sometimes an appropriate response to a negative situation. Try to image your own feelings when you were frustrated or humiliated, or when you could not do something.

Also, consider struggling readers. Since reading is such a prominent part of our K–12 educational system, students who are struggling readers fail in a very public way every day. And they are constantly reminded of their failures. They are sometimes called lazy for not getting homework completed, even though it takes them two hours to read an assignment that it might take 20 minutes for a classmate to read.

Question: When is a learning disability or an emotional/behavioral disorder really a teaching disability or an educational disorder?

Answer: When we try to make the student fit the program, instead of making the program fit the student.

EMOTIONS: AN EVOLUTIONARY PERSPECTIVE

Emotions can be better understood if viewed from an evolutionary perspective. Our current human emotions are a result of thousands of years of human evolution (LeDoux, 2002). They are part of our ever-evolving human brain. As stated above, they are a physiological response to some external stimuli that facilitated actions beneficial for the survival of the group or the individual. We have six basic emotions hardwired into our human brains: anger, fear, surprise, sadness (distress), happiness (joy), and disgust. Each of these served to enable the propagation of our species and the continued spreading of our genes in some fashion.

Think about how each emotion might have promoted behaviors that would benefit early humans or human groups: Anxiety (a type of fear) pushed people to act or plan ahead. Fear prepared them to run or fight. Anger pushed them to protect or respond. Disgust deterred them from eating things or doing things. Joy caused them to do more of certain things. Sadness or distress caused them to do less of things or to do something else.

Even what we might consider to be negative emotions had their place. For example, jealousy, a form of anger, enabled the stabilization of the family unit that was necessary to survive. It is all about the propagation of the species. However, one of the problems with emotions is that some that were hardwired into us to survive in the primitive world may not always serve us well in our modern world.

Fight or Flight

Humans are hardwired not to get eaten by sabertoothed tigers (LeDoux, 2002). Surprise and fear evoke physical reactions that prepare the organism to fight or to run. This is the fight-or-flight response (Ormrod et al., 2020). We see this today in animals as well as humans. Imagine you are walking through the woods. You know there are bears around. Suddenly, you see a large dark shape moving in the brush and hear crashing sounds. Your body automatically responds, going into a state of hyperarousal. Muscles tighten, your eyes widen, your heart rate and blood pressure increase, and your breathing becomes shorter and faster. The three stress hormones are released into your system (cortisol, norepinephrine, and adrenaline).

In this state of hyperarousal, your pupils dilate to allow more light into the eyes and improve your vision. Heart rate and breathing increases to provide your body with the energy and oxygen needed for a quick response. Your skin becomes paled or flushed, indicating that the blood flow to the surface areas of the body is reduced in order to increase the flow to the muscles, brain, legs, and arms. Your muscles become tense and primed for action. You might even lose control of your bladder or bowels so that you do not have to digest food as you are fleeing or fighting. Blood is shunted to the organs critical for your survival (heart, lungs, muscles, brainstem) and away from organs not necessary for your survival (gastrointestinal tract, reproductive tract, immune system, and the prefrontal cortex).

Again, these responses are evolutionary adaptations to increase the chances of survival in dangerous situations. However, in the modern world these responses are not always helpful.

Personal Response to Evolutionary Effect

In our modern world, not all negative events are threats to survival, but our body does not know this (LeDoux, 2015). Physiological responses to negative events or stressful conditions can sometimes cause people to overreact, engage in negative or disruptive thinking, or misinterpret social situations or clues. Reactions of this type that occur overly frequently as well as responses to events that are extreme can be an indication of a mental health condition.

One aspect of mental health is the ability of the mind to right itself or to achieve homeostasis after a stressful event. Mood dysregulation is an inability or difficulty to achieve homeostasis or to regulate the mind after hyperarousal. For example, in response to a stressful situation, a person with a mood dysregulation disorder would get angrier, get angry faster, and stay angry longer when compared to somebody without a mood dysregulation disorder (see Figure 13.1). According to the *Diagnostic and Statistical Manual of Mental Disorders* (DSM-5) (APA, 2013), a disruptive mood dysregulation disorder (DMDD) is characterized by severe recurrent temper outbursts manifested verbally or behaviorally. These outbursts are out of proportion to the situation in terms of the intensity and duration.

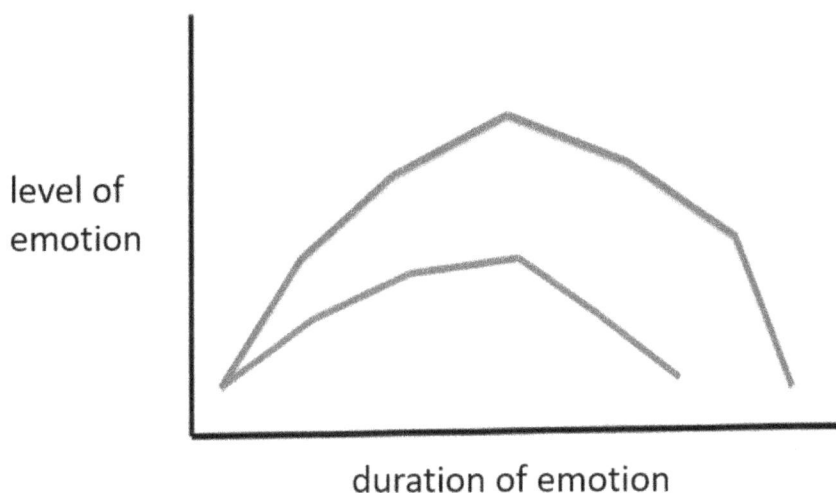

Figure 13.1.   Level and duration of emotions.

Mood dysregulation is also one aspect of an anxiety disorder. According to the DSM-5 (APA, 2013), a generalized anxiety disorder is marked by one or more of the symptoms in Textbox 13.2. Both worry and anger (irritability) are physiological responses based on the fight-or-flight mechanism. In schools, students with mental health conditions such as a mood disorder can be mislabeled as having ADHD, ADD, E/BD, or LD; or as simply being troublesome, lazy, or immature.

**TEXTBOX 13.2. SYMPTOMS OF
GENERALIZED ANXIETY DISORDER**

1. Restlessness or feeling keyed up or on edge
2. Being easily fatigued
3. Difficulty concentrating or mind going blank
4. Irritability
5. Muscle tension
6. Sleep disturbance (difficulty falling or staying asleep, or restless, unsatisfying sleep)

Emotional Influences on Cognitive Functions

The physiological response to fear and anxiety is good for running and fighting, but not so good for learning. When dysregulated, you have less access to your brain's high-level functioning and both perception and memory can be impaired (Gazzaniga et al., 2002). As well, prolonged exposure to stress (chronic stress) makes achieving homeostasis more difficult. And as will be described in more detail Chapter 18, children living in poverty are exposed to more stressful events than students not living in poverty. The chronic stress they experience can make it more difficult for them to turn off the fear switch once the threat is gone. This all makes it less likely that they will come to school ready and able to learn.

Finally, we think, learn, and emote with the same brain. Thus, it would be silly to think that emotions would not be a factor in students' ability to learn. Positive emotional experiences can enhance and promote learning; negative emotions can disrupt and prevent learning (Machazo & Motz, 2005; Sousa, 2011). And since there is plenty of research to support this notion, we can say that attending to students' emotions can be considered a *research-based strategy.*

Part III

COMPLEX THINKING

Chapter Fourteen

Thinking Levels and Skills

BLOOM'S TAXONOMY

Back in 1948, Benjamin Bloom classified intellectual behaviors that were to be used to design three different kinds of lessons: lessons to teach knowledge (the cognitive domain); lessons to teach skills (the psychomotor domain); and lessons to teach attitudes, values, and behaviors (the affective domain) (Hall & Johnson, 1994). Within each domain he created categories or taxonomies (see Table 14.1). These categories were then to be used to design lesson plan objectives. The lesson plan objective (called a behavioral objective) was the intended outcome of the lesson. That is, if learning was to have occurred, students would display a behavior related to one of the categories within the domain.

Table 14.1. Bloom's Taxonomies

Cognitive	Psychomotor	Affective
• knowledge	• observe	• receiving
• comprehension	• model	• responding
• application	• recognize standards	• valuing
• analysis	• correct	• organizing
• synthesis	• apply	• characterizing
• evaluation	• coach	

Bloom's ideas here were much too complicated to be practical. His taxonomies related to psychomotor and affective domains are largely unused today; however, his taxonomy of thinking is still widely used to understand different kinds of thinking.

Six Categories and Two Levels of Thinking

Bloom's taxonomy identifies six different kinds (categories) of thinking. This is a taxonomy of thinking, not a hierarchy. A *taxonomy* is a system for classification. Even though the term "levels" is often used to describe the six categories of thinking, there are only two levels: less-complex thinking and more-complex thinking. Being able to know and comprehend things is considered less-complex thinking (Textbox 14.1). These cognitive operations generally take up less space in working memory and involve fewer component parts when compared to the other categories: applying, analyzing, synthesizing, or evaluating things (see Textbox 14.2).

TEXTBOX 14.1. LESS-COMPLEX COGNITIVE OPERATIONS

Knowledge. Students recall facts or remember previously learned material.

- *Knowledge level operations*: define, describe, identify, list, match, name, tell, describe, show, label, collect, examine, tabulate, quote, duplicate, memorize, recognize, relate, recall, repeat, reproduce, or state

Comprehension. Students grasp the meaning of material. This assumes that there is some level of meaningful learning.

- *Comprehension level operations*: interpret, explain, summarize, convert, defend, distinguish, estimate, generalize, rewrite, contrast, predict, associate, distinguish, estimate, differentiate, discuss, extend, classify, discuss, express, indicate, locate, report, restate, review, select, or translate

Describing the cognitive operations related to knowledge and comprehension as less-complex thinking is not meant to devalue this kind of thinking. This type of thinking is necessary for encoding and then being able to use and apply new information. However, if this is the only type of thinking used for activities, assignments, and discussions, it leads to low levels of learning as students are not able to manipulate concepts deeply. As well, students do not get the opportunities to develop more-complex thinking.

Creating Discussion Questions, Activities, and Assignments

As stated above, Benjamin Bloom originally created this taxonomy to be used to design educational objectives. However, the real value in the taxonomy is not in writing lesson plan objectives. Instead, it is in using the action words

TEXTBOX 14.2. MORE-COMPLEX COGNITIVE OPERATIONS

Application. Students use or apply learned material in a new situation.

- *Application level operations*: apply, change, compute, demonstrate, operate, show, use, solve, calculate, complete, illustrate, examine, modify, relate, change, classify, experiment, dramatize, employ, illustrate, interpret, operate, practice, schedule, sketch, or write

Analysis. Students break things down into parts in order to understand, organize, or clarify.

- *Analysis level operations*: identify parts, distinguish, diagram, outline, relate or associate, break down, discriminate, subdivide, analyze, separate, order, explain, connect, classify, arrange, divide, select, explain, infer, analyze, appraise, calculate, categorize, compare, contrast, criticize, differentiate, discriminate, distinguish, examine, experiment, question, or test

Synthesis. Students put parts together to form a new whole.

- *Synthesis level operations*: combine, compose, create, design, rearrange, integrate, modify, substitute, plan, invent, formulate, prepare, generalize, or rewrite

Evaluation. Using a given criterion, students determine the value of a thing or quality of a product or performance.

- *Evaluation level operations*: appraise, criticize, compare and contrast, support, conclude, discriminate, find main points, explain, infer, deduce, assess, decide, rank, grade, test, measure, recommend, convince, select, judge, explain, discriminate, support, argue, choose, defend, estimate, judge, predict, rate, select, value, or evaluate

for each level to design discussion questions, activities, and assignments (Johnson, 2017). For example, Mr. Manfred's fourth-grade class was reading the original versions of common fairy tales. Using Bloom's taxonomy, he created the following activities for "Little Red Ridinghood."

1. **Knowledge.** Describe how the wolf got into Grandma's house.

2. **Comprehension.** Create a story map that shows the events that happened in this story.

3. **Application.** Create a one-minute mime-drama that shows how the wolf tried to trick Little Red Ridinghood and what happened.

4. **Analysis.** Using a web of comparison, compare and contrast "The Three Little Pigs" and "Little Red Ridinghood."

5. Evaluation. Define four elements of a good story. Rate "Little Red Ridinghood" on each element (evaluation).

6. Synthesis. Combine elements of "The Three Little Pigs" and "Little Red Ridinghood" to create a new story.

These are six different activities based on the cognitive operations listed in Textboxes 14.1 and 14.2. You can see that the possibilities for creating activities, assignments, and discussion questions are many.

THINKING SKILLS

We can enable students to become more proficient thinkers and to master complex cognitive processes by teaching thinking skills and embedding them across the curriculum.

Defining Our Terms

A *thinking skill* is any cognitive process broken down into a set of steps that are then used to guide thinking (Johnson, 2017). For example, supporting a statement or making an argument is a common cognitive process found in many academic standards. Here you use appropriate reasons, detail, or examples to make the case for a declarative statement, an argument, or a conclusion. This cognitive process can be made into a thinking skill by breaking it into the following steps: (a) Look at the statement, (b) gather data to support that statement, (c) organize the data, and (d) describe the statement with supporting data. This process can then be taught explicitly.

Thinking skills are different from complex thinking. As stated above, complex thinking is any cognitive process that places high demands on the thinking and data sorting taking place in working memory. Students benefit little from simply being asked to engage in complex thinking tasks. For example, inference is another common cognitive process found in many academic standards. If a teacher were to simply ask students to make an inference related to some aspect of a story being read, those who are already adept at this complex thinking task would be able to do it easily while other students would become frustrated. This is unfortunately what often happens under the guise of thinking skills "instruction." Teachers just present complex thinking tasks without any instruction whatsoever.

To infer one must integrate observed clues with background knowledge in order to make an informed speculation. This cognitive process can be made into a thinking skill by breaking it into the following steps: (a) Identify the question or point of inference, (b) identify what is known or observed, (c) identify related knowledge that is relevant, and (d) make a reasoned guess based on b and c. With instruction, complex thinking becomes relatively easy. This is the major premise of thinking skills instruction: Complicated things are made easy by breaking them into parts and teaching them explicitly.

Teaching Thinking Skills

Thinking skills should be taught using direct instruction with thinking frames (Johnson, 2000). A thinking frame is a visual representation of the cognitive process broken down into specific steps. Table 14.2 contains the thinking frames for the two thinking skills described earlier. These can be put in poster form and placed in the classroom for teaching and easy review.

Table 14.2. Examples of Thinking Frames

Support a Statement	Infer
1. Look at the statement. 2. Gather data to support the statement. 3. Organize the data. 4. Describe the statement with supporting data.	1. Identify the question or point of inference. 2. Identify what is known or observed. 3. Identify related knowledge that is relevant. 4. Make a reasoned guess based on 2 and 3.

Thinking skills and other forms of complex thinking should be taught, modeled, and practiced in a large group first. For younger students, larger-group instruction, modeling, and practice should take place over many sessions. For older students, fewer sessions will be needed. Eventually students should be asked to use the complex thinking process in small groups or pairs. This provides the scaffolding necessary to use the new skill and enables students to hear the thinking of others. Eventually, students can be engaged in the complex thinking process individually. With younger students, this takes longer. With older students the time needed is shorter.

And, like any new skill, mastery of a thinking skill does not occur after a single encounter. It takes regular practice and review for students to learn and to be able to use it independently. Embedding thinking skills throughout the curriculum provides the necessary context for practice and mastery and it enhances learning by inviting students to interact with content at deeper levels.

CRITICAL AND CREATIVE THINKING

Let us next differentiate between two types of thinking: critical thinking and creative thinking. *Critical thinking* is a type of thinking that converges on a single thought or entity. It is sometimes called convergent thinking. Here one must organize, analyze, or evaluate information. The opposite of critical thinking is *creative thinking*. This is thinking that diverges from a single point or entity. This is sometimes called divergent thinking. Here one must generate, synthesize, find alternatives, adapt, substitute, or elaborate ideas or information. Thinking related to each of these cognitive processes could become thinking skills if the processes were broken into parts and taught explicitly.

Thinking Frames: Critical Thinking Skills

The thinking frames for eight critical thinking skills are outlined in Table 14.3. Each of these can be used to design activities and assignments across the curriculum.

Table 14.3.   Critical Thinking Skills

Skill	Thinking Frame
Inferring: Go beyond the available information to identify what may reasonably be true.	1. Identify the question or point of inference. 2. Identify what is known or observed. 3. Identify related knowledge that is relevant. 4. Make a reasoned guess based on 2 and 3.
Decision-Making: Examine the options and alternatives in order to decide on a course of action.	1. Identify the problem or decision. 2. Generate decision options. 3. Evaluate costs and rewards of options. 4. Make a choice based on the above.
Compare and Contrast: Find similarities and differences between/among two or more items.	1. Look at all items. 2. Find the similarities. 3. Find the differences. 4. Conclude and describe.
Ordering: Arrange events, concepts, or items in sequential order based on a criterion.	1. Look at or define a criterion. 2. Look at the whole. 3. Arrange items within the whole according to the criterion. 4. Describe the whole in terms of the new order.
Analyze: Break an item or event down into its component parts.	1. Look at the item or event. 2. Identify important parts. 3. Describe each part. 4. Describe the whole in terms of each part.

Skill	Thinking Frame
Evaluation/Critique: Make a formal critique based on a set of criteria.	1. Look at or define a criterion. 2. Look at the subject. 3. Compare the subject to the criterion. 4. Describe the subject relative to the criterion.
Supporting a Statement: Use appropriate reasons, detail, or examples to support a statement, idea, or conclusion.	1. Look at the statement. 2. Gather data to support the statement. 3. Organize the data 4. Describe the statement with supporting data.
Creating Groups (Inductive Analysis): Impose order on a field by identifying and grouping common themes or patterns.	1. Look at the whole. 2. Identify reoccurring items, themes, or patterns. 3. Arrange into groups. 4. Describe the whole in terms of groups.

Thinking Frames: Creative Thinking Skills

The thinking frames for seven creative thinking skills are outlined in Table 14.4. Each of these can also be used to design activities and assignments across the curriculum.

Table 14.4. Thinking Frames for Creative Thinking Skills

Skill	Thinking Frame
Fluency: Generate as many ideas as possible without evaluating.	1. Look at the idea or problem. 2. Do not worry about good or bad ideas. 3. Add as many ideas as quickly as you can.
Integrate: Connect, combine, or synthesize two or more things to form a new whole.	1. Look at all things. 2. Select interesting or important parts from each. 3. Combine to describe a new whole.
Flexibility: Create a variety of different approaches.	1. Look at the original. 2. Find other ways for it to be used, solved, or applied.
Brainstorming Web: Create a web to generate ideas relative to a given topic.	1. Look at the original ideas. 2. Analyze to identify two to five related ideas for subheadings. 3. Brainstorm to generate ideas for each subheading. 4. Describe.
Elaboration: Embellish an original idea.	1. Look at the idea. 2. Add things to it to make it better or more interesting.

(continued)

Table 14.4. *(continued)*

Skill	Thinking Frame
Generating Relationships: The student will find related items or events.	1. Look at the item or event. 2. Generate attributes. 3. Find items or events with similar or related attributes. 4. Describe the relationship.
Originality: Create new ideas that are unusual or unique.	1. Find an idea or problem. 2. Think of solutions or applications that nobody else has thought of before.

Chapter Fifteen

Problem-Solving

PROBLEMS

Problem-solving is another form of complex thinking. And just like thinking skills, we can help students to become more proficient problem solvers by teaching problem-solving skills and by including problems in all curriculum areas (problem-based learning).

Defining Our Terms

A *problem* is a situation in which the present condition, product, or performance does not match the desired condition, product, or performance. Problem-solving is a matter of moving from the present to the desired. As you will see below, problem-solving involves both creative thinking (the ability to generate a lot of ideas) and critical thinking (the ability to analyze and evaluate ideas). Effective problem solvers are able to do both. Ineffective problem solvers are usually only able to focus on one kind of thinking.

Types of Problems

There are two types of problems: well-structured and ill-structured. *Well-structured problems* are easily defined, all the information needed to solve the problem is available, and there is a single solution. These are the kinds of problems found in computer science or math, or the logic problems found on intelligence tests (see Table 15.1). Math problems found in the context of a paragraph are called word problems. We can help students get better at these by teaching the process using a thinking frame (see Textbox 15.1). This should be part of math instruction at all levels and should be reviewed each year.

Table 15.1. Examples Of Well-Structured and Ill-Structured Problems

Well-Structured Problems	Ill-Structured Problems
• Sara has 15 apples and 12 oranges. How many pieces of fruit does she have?	• Billy is mean to me.
	• I am nervous about tests.
	• My roommate is a slob.
• Mari has 15 apples and 3 times as many oranges. How many pieces of fruit does she have?	• How can I keep my seventh-grade social studies class be interested and engaged?
• Two consecutive numbers have a sum of 91. What are the numbers?	• I want to develop a relationship with . . .
• Two numbers have a sum of 87. The larger of the numbers is twice that of the smaller. What are the numbers?	• I want to read at night, but my wife is bothered by the light.
• $[6 - (4 - 5(5 - 3) + 2)] + 2$	• How do I explain complex thinking in a way that is easy to understand?
	• How do I fix my bike?

TEXTBOX 15.1. THINKING FRAME FOR WORD PROBLEMS

1. Read the problem.
2. Record important information.
3. Use pictures or diagrams if needed.
4. Decide on the operation(s).
5. Solve the problem.
6. Check your answer.

The problem with well-structured problems is that they do not reflect reality. Reality is ill-structured, not well-structured. *Ill-structured problems* are the types of problems most often encountered in our ill-structured real world. Here, all the needed information is often not present and there is not a single answer or solution to the problem.

SOLVING PROBLEMS

As stated in Chapter 11, the first step in solving a problem is perceiving a problem. Teachers can help students begin to perceive problems by helping them recognize the discrepancy between the real and the ideal. The graphic organizer in Figure 15.1 can be used here.

After perceiving a problem, the next step is to select a problem-solving strategy. There are two types of problem-solving strategies: algorithms and heuristics. An *algorithm* is a step-by-step set of procedures designed to lead

Problem Finder

Current State	Desired State

Figure 15.1. Problem finder.

you to a specific answer. If you follow the steps exactly, you can be guaranteed that you will get to the correct answer. These are great for solving well-structured problems. However, since life is messy and ill-structured, algorithms are of limited use in real-world settings. When people attempt to use algorithms to solve ill-structured problems, the outcome is rarely successful.

The second type of problem-solving strategy is a *heuristic*. These are a general set of steps to get you to a possible solution. While the solutions are not guaranteed, heuristic strategies are more flexible and efficient for solving real-world problems. When people use heuristics to solve ill-structured problems they are much more likely to be successful than when algorithms are used.

Described below are two simple problem-solving heuristics. These will work with most problems encountered in the real, ill-structured world in which we exist.

Creative problem-solving. Creative problem-solving (CPS) is a heuristic that utilizes both critical and creative thinking. After defining the problem, you first generate as many ideas as possible, then you analyze and select the idea that seems best. The thinking frames in Table 15.2 shows three versions of this simple problem-solving heuristic. Table 15.3 includes graphic organizers that can be used to provide a scaffold for students' thinking as you are teaching.

Table 15.2. Thinking Frames for CPS

A Very Simple Version	Basic CPS	A More Complex Version
1. Define the problem.	1. Define the problem.	1. Define the problem.
2. Generate as many ideas as possible.	2. Generate as many ideas as possible.	2. Get background information.
3. Choose an idea that seems the best.	3. Choose an idea that seems the best.	3. Generate as many ideas as possible.
	4. Elaborate and refine.	4. Choose an idea.
		5. Elaborate and refine.

Table 15.3. Graphic Organizers for CPS

Problem
Generate ideas:
Best idea:
Problem
Generate ideas:
Best idea:
Problem
Generate ideas:
Best idea:

Means–ends analysis. Means–ends analysis is a second heuristic problem-solving strategy. Here you first identify the current state, then define the end state or goal. Next, you generate a list of steps necessary to get from the current to the desired (see Table 15.4). Some might add a fourth step, which would be to analyze each of the steps and prioritize them in terms of implementation chronology. The graphic organizers in Table 15.5 can be used as a scaffold here.

Table 15.4. Thinking Frames for MEA

Basic MEA	MEA with a Fourth Step
Thinking Frame	**Thinking Frame**
1. Identify the current state.	1. Identify the current state.
2. Describe the desired state or goal.	2. Describe the desired state or goal.
3. Generate a list of necessary steps or things to do.	3. Generate a list of necessary steps or things to do.
	4. Prioritize and order the steps.

Table 15.5. MEA Graphic Organizers

Current State:	
Goal/End State:	
Necessary Steps/Things to Do: 1. 2. 3. 4. 5.	

Current State:	
Goal/End State:	
Necessary Steps/Things to Do: 1. 2. 3. 4. 5.	Prioritization: 1. 2. 3. 4. 5.

Brainstorming

As stated above, effective problem solvers utilize two types of thinking: (a) creative or divergent thinking and (b) critical or convergent thinking. Excluding either type of thinking leads to ineffective problem-solving. Brainstorming is a strategy that can help with creative thinking. The rules were described in Chapter 11.

We cannot assume that students (or adults) know how to brainstorm. The brainstorming rules should be taught explicitly and posted in classrooms as well as any professional setting where problem-solving occurs (see Textbox 15.2).

TEXTBOX 15.2. RULES FOR BRAINSTORMING

1. All ideas must be accepted.
2. Freewheeling is celebrated.
3. The goal of brainstorming is quantity.
4. Hitchhiking is welcome.

Things That Get in the Way

Besides not knowing basic problem-solving strategies, there are five other things that can get in the way of effective problem-solving:

1. Functional fixedness. This is the inability to see a use for an object other than how it is usually used. Your way of thinking about the function of something is fixed or locked in. In a classic experiment, Duncker (1945) gave participants a candle, a box of thumbtacks, and a book of matches. They were asked to attach the candle to the wall in a way that wax would not drip on the table below. Most participants tried to attach the candle to the wall using the tacks or using the melted wax as glue. Very few considered using the box in which the thumbtacks came as a candleholder. Once the box was attached to the wall using the thumbtacks, it could become a candle holder to keep the wax from dripping on the table. Most participants were fixated on the box's normal function, which was to hold thumbtacks. They could not see another use for it.

2. Mental set. A mental set (sometimes called a response set) is a tendency to perceive only those solutions that have worked in the past. In other words, something has worked in the past, thus, that is the only solution to a new problem, regardless of whether the past solution was the best solution to the problem. As an example, for many years students who demonstrated negative behavior at Mooseville Elementary School were punished. This practice had limited impact, but since it was the only solution ever used, it was the only solution considered to address classroom management problems. The only alternative question was, how to punish students. Other ideas such as looking at the cause of the negative behavior or focusing on positive behaviors were never considered.

3. Cross-domain problem-solving. Here you identify a solution that has worked in one domain and apply it to another domain. This is common in education when business leaders are called in to advise on educational matters (although education leaders are rarely asked to advise on business matters). The thinking is that those solutions that worked in a business setting, where profits are the bottom line, will work in education, where people are the bottom line. The results of this kind of cross-domain problem-solving are rarely good, especially when it comes to education.

4. Brain drought. This is the inability or unwillingness to generate ideas. In other words, problem solvers do not know the rules of brainstorming.

5. Lack of knowledge. Knowledge related to the problem being solved is necessary. It provides greater perspectives, more options, and a better sense of consequences of various options. It is very hard to be an effective problem solver with a limited knowledge. For example, Dr. Johnson is a professor whose expertise is in literacy instruction. He is able to solve all sorts of problems related to the teaching of reading and struggling readers. But when asked to solve problems related to finance or business, he is of little use.

Problem-Based Learning

Problem-based learning is inserting problems into the curriculum. Teachers can insert curriculum-related problems in two ways: The first is to simply present a problem related to lesson content as a post-lesson activity. This enables students to build upon, expand, or reinforce what has been learned and to engage with learned content more deeply by using more complex thinking. For example, in reading or literature, as a post-reading activity students could be asked to solve problems that characters face or to solve similar story problems that they may have encountered in their lives. In other content areas, students can be presented with ill-structured problems related to the topics being studied.

The second way to use problems in a curriculum is to use them as a form of discovery learning. Here students would be asked to solve a problem related to lesson content before the lesson. This would enable them to learn about or discover important knowledge and skills ahead of the lesson. The teacher would then use instruction to fill in the blanks during the lesson.

Problem-Solving for Personal and Interpersonal Problems

Finally, problem-solving strategies can be used to help students address personal and interpersonal problems. This works best if students are asked to find solutions for these problems in cooperative learning groups of three to six students. (Use smaller group sizes for younger students and larger for older students.) The small-group setting enables students to hear a variety of alternatives as well as the thinking of other students.

Of course, to find problems for students, you must know your students. That is, you must know the types of problems they may be facing. These may be problems related to drugs, friends, bullying, parents, sex, or other common issues. By presenting these as somebody else's problems, or problems faced by a fictitious character, students are more comfortable exploring similar problems in their own lives. Here they are addressing the problems of somebody else who is going through similar situations that they might be facing or will face. The small group provides a safe environment to explore options and alternatives.

There are five ways to identify appropriate personal and interpersonal problems for students to address.

1. Media and current events. Look for relevant problems in books students are reading, as well as TV programs, movies, newspapers, or current events.

2. Common problems. Look for common personal and interpersonal problems that your students might face. These could be common problems student their age face or common problems found at school or in the community.

3. Dear Abby and other advice columns. Advice columns are a great source to use in finding relevant problems to solve. As well, groups can compare their advice to that given by the advice columnist. Again, discretion and a thorough knowledge of your students should be used in selecting the types of problems to be examined here.

4. Anonymous volunteer-in-a-problem box. Here, students would be encouraged to anonymously submit a personal problem in a problem box to use with small groups. You would need to use a word processor to make edits before distributing the problem to small groups in order to avoid potentially embarrassing the student or inappropriate disclosure. This can be a powerful learning activity; however, again you must use your discretion and knowledge of your students to guide you here. This also can become a vehicle for you to use to discuss issues related to friendship, trust, keeping confidences, and talking about personal issues.

5. Students choose problems. Students could choose problems to bring to small groups. A great amount of caution and discretion should be used here. This is not something you would do the first month of a school year. You need to know your students and a high level of trust and respect for classmates must be built before students do this. Also, remind students to only bring problems that they feel comfortable sharing and talking about in small groups. There are other times and places to talk about more personal issues.

Chapter Sixteen

Metacognition, Study Skills Strategies, Comprehension Skills, and Note-Taking

This chapter will focus on four variations of complex thinking: (a) metacognition, (b) study skills strategies, (c) comprehension skills, and (d) note-taking. To review, *complex thinking* is any cognitive process that places high demands on the thinking and data sorting taking place in working memory.

METACOGNITION

Metacognition means thinking about thinking or monitoring one's thought process. This term is usually associated with reading comprehension. Here a reader pauses and asks, "Do I understand what I just read?" "Does what I just read make sense?" If not, the expert readers employ some sort of fix-up strategy. The study skill strategy in Textbox 16.1 is an example of metacognition that can be taught using direct instruction and cognitive modeling.

TEXTBOX 16.1. THINKING FRAME FOR METACOGNITIVE READING STRATEGY

1. Read a paragraph.
2. Pause and check. (Do I understand?)
3. Return or resume.

The reader might also ask, "How is this related to what I already know?"

STUDY SKILLS STRATEGIES

Study skills strategies are procedures that a reader consciously employs to help create meaning with textbooks and other informational reading material (Johnson, 2016). We must teach students to use these. However, if we want students to actually use them, they must be simple, pragmatic, and effective. This section describes six such study skills strategies that can be used by students at all levels.

Simple Study Skills Strategies

- **Basic note-taking.** We can never assume that students know this basic study skill strategy (see Textbox 16.2). This basic note-taking strategy will be sufficient for most study situations students will encounter in middle school, high school, and beyond. Some form of this should be taught and reinforced every year. Keep this simple as students will naturally develop more complex forms of note-taking as the need arises.

TEXTBOX 16.2. A BASIC NOTE-TAKING STRATEGY

1. Write the title of the article or chapter at the top of the page.
2. Write the name of the headings (underlined) as you encounter them.
3. Read each paragraph and find just the important ideas.
4. Record ideas using short, abbreviated (incomplete) sentences.
5. Record supporting ideas below sentences.
   a. Use numerals for main ideas.
   b. Use small letters for supporting ideas.

- **Read, dot, and record.** For this study skill strategy, put a dot in the margin of the text with a pencil to note important ideas as you are reading. (You can go back and erase the dots later.) This enables you to continue reading without interrupting the reading flow. After reading, go back and take notes using your dots.
- **Preview-overview.** Start by reading the first paragraph and the last paragraph. Preview headings. Then read the entire text and take notes.
- **Read and pause.** Read a paragraph. Then pause to see if you understood and can restate an important idea. If so, resume reading. If not, return and reread (see above).
- **Paragraph reread.** Read a paragraph. Then skim to find an important idea. Continue.

- **3 × 5 card.** A 3 × 5 card helps to keep you focused as you read. Put the card underneath the line you are reading. This can also be used in conjunction with any of the strategies described above.

Never Assume

You can never assume that students at any level know how to read textbooks and other informational material. Thus, two or three study skills strategies should be taught each year. Keep it simple and practical. Adopt and adapt. Encourage students to use the ones that work best for them. Also, create posters with the study skills strategies that you will teach. Use these as a reference (see Table 16.1). And when assigning a textbook or other informational material, always remind students to use one of these study skills strategies.

Table 16.1. Poster Ideas for Study Skills Strategies

Take Notes	Dot and Notes	Preview/Overview
1. Record headings. 2. Read a paragraph. 3. Record important ideas. 4. Use numbers and letters.	1. Read a paragraph. 2. Put dots next to important ideas. 3. Finish a chapter. 4. Take notes using outline and headings.	1. Look at the title and headings. 2. Read the first paragraph and last paragraph. 3. Read the article/chapter. 4. Take notes.
Paragraph Reread	*3 × 5 Card*	*Read and Pause*
1. Read each paragraph quickly. 2. Reread to find important sentences or ideas. 3. Continue.	1. Put a card on top/bottom of sentence. 2. Move slowly ahead as you read.	1. Read a paragraph. 2. Pause and check. (Do I understand?) 3. Return or resume.

COMPREHENSION SKILLS

Here we must differentiate between a strategy and a skill. A *strategy* is a cognitive process that one consciously applies to a task (Johnson, 2021). This is what a study skill strategy is (see above). A *skill* in terms of complex thinking is a cognitive process that has become automated. That is, you do not have to think about it. When teaching complex thinking, the goal is always automaticity. That is, we want students to engage in the complex thinking processes automatically, without having to think about them. It is the same with comprehension skills.

Comprehending Narrative and Expository Text

To address comprehension skills, we must first understand that there are two different types of text (Johnson, 2016). *Narrative texts* are descriptions of events. These include fiction such as fairytales, plays, fantasy, detective stories, thrillers, science fiction, or romance. It also includes nonfiction such as biographies, autobiographies, memoirs, diaries, or personal recollections. *Expository texts* describe information and ideas. This could include things such as informational books, articles, editorials, encyclopedias, websites, dictionaries, manuals, directions, magazines, or newspapers. Efficient readers approach narrative and expository text differently (Allington & McGill-Franzen, 2009). The study skills strategies above should only be used with expository text. Narrative text must be approached slightly differently and use comprehension skills.

Comprehension is a cognitive process. Comprehension with narrative text can be improved by improving thinking (Johnson, 2016). This is done by teaching the cognitive operations in Textbox 16.3 and then using them to design pre-, during-, and post-reading activities. It is beyond the scope of this text to elaborate further here. However, this is described in *Designing Meaning-Based Interventions for Reading* (Johnson, 2021) and *10 Essential Instructional Elements for Students with Reading Difficulties: A Brain-Friendly Approach* (Johnson, 2016).

TEXTBOX 16.3. COGNITIVE OPERATIONS USED BY EFFECTIVE READERS

1. compare
2. respond aesthetically
3. infer
4. identify important ideas or themes
5. identify supporting details
6. identify cause-effect relationships
7. problem solve
8. analyze
9. evaluate
10. make connections
11. order
12. use inductive analysis
13. predict
14. recognize story grammar
15. reflect using metacognition
16. visualize
17. question
18. summarize

NOTE-TAKING

Note-taking during lectures (as well as reading) enhances understanding and remembering (encoding and retrieval). Just like the study skills strategies above, we cannot assume that students at any level know why it is important and how to do it.

Why It Is Important

There are four reasons why it is important to take notes during class lectures:

1. To stay actively engaged. First, note-taking keeps you actively engaged. Humans do not learn passively. We are not like computers. We cannot simply absorb new information with input. We must be engaged with new information we encounter at some level. The more active our engagement, the better we are able to understand and remember the new information. The act of analyzing this new information, looking for important ideas, and then physically recording them on paper keeps us actively engaged.

2. To apply levels of processing theory. Levels of processing theory states that our memory varies according to the level or amount of processing that takes place during encoding. In other words, if you do something with new information, you are more likely to remember it. The act of looking for important ideas and physically taking notes during lectures necessitates that you process new information at deeper levels than you would by simply listening.

3. To extend short-term memory. Notes create a visual representation of short-term memory. This is important because short-term memory can hold approximately seven plus or minus two bits of information for about 15 seconds. That is not a lot of information and that is of short duration. Paper (or a computer screen) enables you to visually see a lot more information without taxing the limited amount of space in short-term memory. And when you take notes you can easily see how one thing relates to another. As well, the new information on the page does not begin to fade after 15 seconds.

4. To avoid rote learning. Rote learning is when you take in new information that is unrelated to anything else. Taking notes during lectures enables you to record your own ideas and associations along with new information.

Basic Note-Taking Strategy for Lectures and Learning

There are a variety of forms and strategies that students can use. Textbox 16.4 contains a basic note-taking strategy that will work for most lecture situations.

TEXTBOX 16.4. BASIC NOTE-TAKING STRATEGY FOR LECTURES

1. Look for interesting or important ideas.
2. Record using short, abbreviated sentences.
3. Enumerate (use numbers) for new ideas.
4. Use underlined topic headings.
5. Use new headings for new topics.

Preparing for Exams

Exams are a fact of educational life. Two strategies are described here to enhance learning and at the same time enable students to perform better on exams:

Synthesize and organize your notes. First, synthesize and organize the information from class lectures and assigned readings so that all the ideas are found in one place and under common headings. This process requires that you evaluate and analyze this information. These two complex thinking processes enhance understanding and memory.

For example, Professor Johnson allowed his students to type up and use two pages of notes (single-sided) for class exams. He encouraged them to use 10-point font and two columns on each page (so they could get more information on the page) and to also use highlighters to indicate topic headings. The process of selecting and synthesizing relevant information to fit into the two-page format required complex thinking. As a result, most students found that their notes were largely unnecessary when taking the exam.

Use study groups. The second idea is to form a study group. In pairs or small groups, take turns explaining the ideas from class and the assigned reading to each other. Explaining these ideas in your own words or reteaching these new concepts requires you to analyze the information and understand it at deeper levels. Also, hearing other people's explanation of key ideas and concepts often enhances and expands your own understanding.

Chapter Seventeen

Conceptual Understanding and Transfer

The last two areas of complex thinking examined here are understanding and transferring concepts.

CONCEPTUAL LEARNING

Humans have an innate desire to make sense of their environment (Bruner, 1977). When we experience reality, the human brain naturally seeks to induce order from it. One way it does this is by noticing reoccurring patterns and creating categories based on those patterns (Bruner, 1966). This cognitive operation is called *inductive reasoning*. Here interpretations and understandings are developed based on a broad array of data observed in a large field. *Deductive reasoning* is a complimentary cognitive process where a specific conclusion is made based on a limited set of data. Whereas deductive reasoning uses bits of data to identify a specific answer (Sherlock Holmes type of thinking), inductive reasoning uses reoccurring patterns found in a larger field to identify hypotheses or form new understandings (Margaret Mead type of thinking). Both types of reasoning are used when forming new concepts.

Categories and Concepts

A *category* is a classification of objects or entities based on common properties. It is a group of things that are the same in some way. A *concept* is a type of category that has defining attributes that identify specific elements necessary for an entity to be an example of that group.

These are some examples of concepts: triangle, square, parallel, perpendicular, poker, mammal, liberal, paragraph, immigrant, gravitas, intuition, expository text, a declarative statement, myth, compassion, labor union, justice, democracy. Some concepts are clearly defined, such as triangle, mammal, proper nouns, and alliteration. You can say yes or no as to whether an entity is an example of that concept. Other concepts have fuzzy edges, such as equity, religion, liberal, democracy, religion, or truck. Identifying conceptual examples is not always clear cut.

Identifying Concepts

Below are three cognitive operations we use to identify concepts (Eggen & Kaucheck, 2013). Understanding these cognitive processes informs how we should teach concepts.

Rule-driven analysis. Concepts are sometimes identified by comparing an entity to a set of *defining attributes*. Defining attributes are the features required for the entity to be a concept. For example, the defining attributes of an amphibian are (a) it is born with gills, (b) it grows lungs, (c) it lays its eggs in water, (d) it is cold-blooded, (e) it can walk on land, and (f) it hibernates. Using rule-driven analysis for amphibians, we would compare creatures to the six defining attributes to determine if they are amphibians.

Teaching new concepts using rule-driven analysis starts with teaching the defining attributes. Attribute charts are commonly used here. These are graphic organizers for teaching new concepts that enable students to easily compare entities and attributes (Table 17.1).

Table 17.1. Amphibian Attribute Chart

	born with gills	grow lungs	lay eggs in water	cold-blooded	walks on land	hibernates
snake	x	x		x	x	x
turtle	x	x		x	x	x
sunfish	x		x	x		
from	x	x	x	x	x	x
lizard		x		x	x	x
bear					x	x
salamander	x	x	x	x	x	x

Exemplar comparison. Here concepts are identified by comparing the entity to all the other examples of that entity (exemplars) stored in our memory. When teaching new concepts, students may have examples already stored in memory without realizing that they are examples of that concept. For example, when teaching the concept of reptiles, students most likely have some examples of reptiles stored in their memory without realizing that they are reptiles. Other times the teacher must provide many examples of the concept for comparison. For example, a ninth-grade teacher teaching the concept of onomatopoeia for the first time would need to provide many examples for students to use for making comparisons.

Prototype matching. A prototype is the best example of a concept that is stored in our memory. Here all the defining attributes of the concept are present and clearly articulated. Prototypes are developed by assimilating the essential features of all the examples of the concept stored in our memory. Prototype matching is the cognitive process in which we identify concepts by comparing entities to a prototypical example of that concept. When teaching a new concept, it is helpful to provide a prototypical example in which all the defining features are evident and articulated.

Teaching Concepts

Learning a concept involves being able to identify its defining attributes as well as to distinguish between valid and invalid examples of the concept. Concepts can be taught using direct instruction or some form of discovery learning (Johnson, 2019):

Direct instruction. Direct instruction is a teacher-centered approach in which the information is presented to students in its final form (Johnson, 2019). These are the steps for using direct instruction to teach concepts:

1. Present a definition of the concept using words with which students are familiar.
2. Present the defining attributes of the concepts. Tell students that in order for the entity to be the concept it must have all of the defining attributes. *Concept maps,* sometimes called semantic maps, can be used here (Johnson, 2017). These are any type of visual representation of a concept that shows the relationship among ordinate and subordinate parts (see Figure 17.1).
3. Present many examples of the concept. With each example, emphasize the defining attributes (tell why the concept is the concept).
4. Present near-examples of the concept. Show examples of things that are similar but are not the concept. Use the defining attributes to describe why each example is not the concept. (Remember that all the defining attributes must be present for it to be the concept.)
5. Using guided practice, ask students to identify concepts. Present both positive and negative examples to students. They should use deductive reasoning to identify each and tell why it is or is not the concept.
6. Use independent practice to reinforce concept learning. Here students practice what they have already learned related to the new concept. Independent practice can be done individually or in small groups.

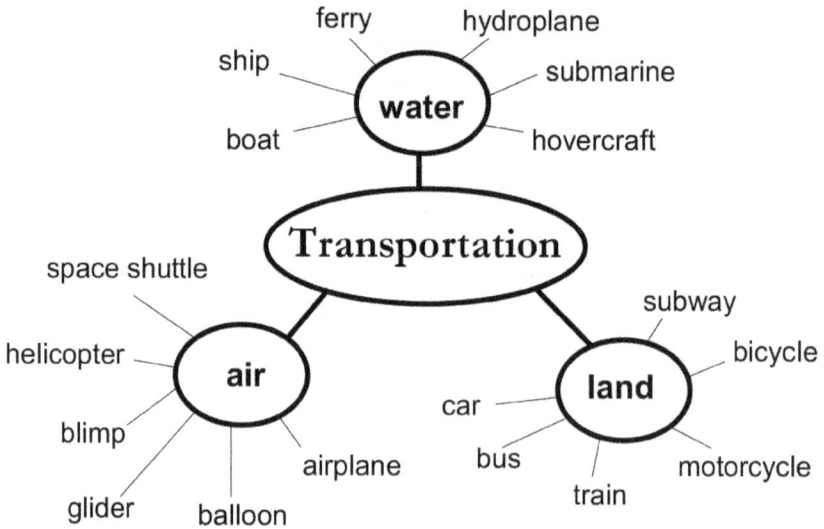

Figure 17.1.   Concept map.

Discovery learning. Using discovery learning, students are asked to use inductive reasoning to determine the defining attributes of a concept. These are the basic steps for using discovery learning for teaching concepts:

1. Provide students with several examples of the concept. Ask them if they can perceive any similarities or common attributes.
2. Provided non-examples or near-examples. Ask students to compare them with examples and note differences.
3. Ask students to postulate what might be the defining attributes of the concept.
4. Present the name and definition of the concept.
5. Make corrections or additions to students' list of defining attributes.
6. As a form of guided practice, ask students to identify other examples and non-examples of the concept. They should be able to summarize principles or main concepts at this point.
7. Create a concept map or graphic organizer at the end of the lesson to describe and illustrate the concept.

TRANSFER OF LEARNING

The last area of complex thinking we will examine is transfer of learning. Transfer is the ability to take what is learned in one setting and use it in new situations (Mayer & Wittrock, 2006). If students cannot use their learning outside of a school context, it is of little use.

Near and Far

Transfer can be near or far.

Near transfer. *Near transfer* occurs when new learning is applied to situations that resemble that in which it was learned. That is, when students are able to use what they learned in conditions that are similar to initial learning. Transfer here occurs quite easily. For example, pilots train in a flight simulator. The goal is to make the initial learning very much like the conditions in which they will be using that learning. Also, if somebody learns how to fix a computer or a car in one setting, this type of learning generally resembles the situation in which it will be used and transfer occurs quite easily. Teaching a child how to tie a shoe is another example of a skill in which the initial learning would be almost identical to most shoe-tying situations.

Far transfer. *Far transfer* occurs when new learning is used in situations that are very much different from that in which it was learned. Transfer here is a bit more difficult. For example, learning grammar skills in isolation using sentence diagraming and worksheets is different from most real-life writing situations. This makes transfer of learning more difficult. Another example is that learning in education instructional methods courses in a college classroom does not always resemble the K–12 classroom conditions in which they will be used. This also makes the transfer of learning difficult. The more dissimilar the application conditions are to initial learning conditions, the more difficult it is for the transfer of learning to occur.

Low and High

Transfer of learning can also be low-road or high-road.

Low-road transfer. *Low-road transfer* occurs when the transfer of learning occurs automatically. This usually occurs with low-level skills or basic knowledge. Here students can use their learning in new contexts without thinking. This occurs usually with highly practiced skills and routines. We have students practice in one setting so that they can apply the skill automatically, without thinking, in another setting. For example, when learning to play a clarinet, lots of practice enables the musician to not have to think about fingerings when playing. In sports, coaches do a lot of drills during practice so that athletes are able to perform skills or run the plays without thinking. Lots of reading practice enables students to be able to identify words or engage in cognitive process automatically. Being able to apply a skill automatically (automaticity) frees up working memory for focus on more complex thinking tasks.

Low-road transfer is facilitated using a strategy called *hugging*. This involves extensive practice of skills in a variety of settings. This leads to an automatic triggering of newly learned skills and routines in contexts similar to that in which the initial learning took place. In other words, students can react or respond without thinking.

High-road transfer. *High-road transfer* occurs when a person must use conscious intent to transfer new learning to new contexts. This usually occurs with more complex learning. A good example of this would be the transfer that must take place with the theories of learning and human development described in this book. It will take conscious effort to apply these concepts in the context of the classroom or other real-life settings. However, if you fully understand the guiding principles behind these theories, high-road transfer will occur more readily.

High-road transfer is facilitated by using a strategy called *bridging*. Bridging calls for the teacher to make the bridge from the learning context to the real world using simulations, problem-solving with real-life examples, or asking students to make personal connections and applications to new learning. Bridging also involves teaching for deep understanding so that learners fully comprehend the guiding principles behind new concepts and skills. Bridging enables students to consciously apply high-level skills and concepts in a variety of new contexts.

Promoting Transfer

At some point students will need to travel outside the school environment and use their learning in the real world. So, what can we do to promote transfer? Below are five ideas:

1. **Hugging and bridging.** Use both hugging and bridging when teaching new knowledge and skills (see above).
2. **Personal connections.** Connect new learning to students' lives and experiences.
3. **Real-world applications.** Create conditions in which new learning resembles how it will be used in the real world to the greatest degree possible. This calls for the use of simulations, problem-based learning, and project-based learning. Also, teach skills in authentic contexts to the greatest degree possible. For example, teach the mechanics of writing in the context of students' authentic writing. Teach reading skills in the context of authentic reading situations.

4. **Depth of initial learning.** Teach for deep learning. If the initial learning is shallow and disjointed, transfer is difficult. Having a depth of knowledge related to new learning enhances transfer. Thus, teaching fewer things in-depth is more effective for learning than trying to cover a lot of things superficially.
5. **Practice new learning.** Provide multiple opportunities for students to practice new learning, over time and in a variety of contexts.

Part IV

HUMAN DIVERSITY

Chapter Eighteen

Poverty

This chapter looks at living in poverty and the impact this has on children's ability to learn in school.

LOW SOCIOECONOMIC STATUS

Poverty is a condition in which people do not have the resources necessary to provide life's basic needs such as clean water, food, shelter, and clothing. Depending on the country, you could also include inadequate education, health care, and transportation (World Vision, 2021). There are three kinds of poverty: *Relative poverty* is where people do not enjoy a certain minimal level of living standards as defined by their government. *Situational poverty* is temporary, caused by a sudden crisis such as death, disaster, divorce, or illness. *Absolute poverty* is where people cannot obtain adequate resources to support a minimum level of physical health.

How Common Is Poverty?

According to a United Nations pre-pandemic report, 10% of the world is living in extreme poverty (UN, 2021). There are over 700 million people struggling to get their most basic needs met such as access to water and sanitation, health care, and education. One out of five children live in extreme poverty. And for every 100 men ages 25–34 living in extreme poverty, there are 125 women.

In the United States, 11.1% of the population (38 million people) live in poverty (US Census Bureau, 2021), and 39% of all children live in *low-income families* (NCCP, 2021). Low-income families are defined as those earning less than twice the federal poverty line. For example, if the federal poverty line was an income of $25,000 a year, a low-income family would be a family whose total income was below $50,000. Table 18.1 shows this poverty data broken down by race.

Table 18.1.　U.S. Poverty Data Broken Down by Race

	People Living in Poverty	*Low-Income Households*
Asian	10.1%	27%
White	10.1%	27%
Hispanic	17.6%	56%
Black	20.8%	59%
Total	**11.1%**	**39%**

Children

In 2019, 14.4% of all children under the age of 18 in the United States were living below the official poverty measure (Center for American Progress, 2021) (see Table 18.2). Children living in poverty are more apt to have experienced undernutrition during pregnancy and suffer hunger or malnutrition during the pre-school and school years (Bowe, 2005; Park et al., 2002). This impacts their cognitive development and school performance (Jensen, 2009; Salend, 2004). Some of the effects of an insufficient diet on children in school are fatigue, irritability, inability to concentrate, and frequent colds (Park et al., 2002). Also, children living in poverty have more health problems and are less likely to receive medical care (Jensen, 2013; Park et al., 2002). As well, children living in poverty often live in substandard housing, and are more likely to be victims of child abuse and neglect (Salend, 2004). All of this means that these children will be less likely to come to school each day ready or able to learn (Jensen, 2009; Ormrod et al., 2020).

Table 18.2.　Percentage of U.S. Children Below 18 Living in Poverty

Asian	10%
White	11%
Hispanic	25%
American Indian	31%
Black	32%
Total	**14.4%**

Academic Skills

In their homes, young children living in poverty have less access to books and social networks and are less apt to have computers (Borich, 2004). They are also less likely to have acquired knowledge of the world outside their home or neighborhood. As a result of these and other factors, children living in poverty enter kindergarten and first grade with lower verbal, reading, and math skills than their peers (Park et al., 2002; Salend, 2004). By the end of third grade, they have made smaller gains than other children (NCES, 2019). These students are more apt to fail in school or to be recommended for placement in remedial or special education programs (Salend, 2004). They are also more likely to drop out of high school than their peers not living in poverty (Rumberge, 2013; Bowe, 2005).

Students living in poverty tend to attend schools that receive significantly less state and local money than other schools (U.S. Department of Education, 2021). As a result, they are more apt to be taught in overcrowded, underequipped classrooms (Eggen & Kauchak, 2013). Students living in poverty are also more apt to be taught by unlicensed, out-of-field, or inexperienced teachers (Haycock & Crawford, 2008). Thus, even though the curriculums and programs might be exactly the same, students living in poverty are disadvantaged from the start when compared to students who attend schools in wealthier communities simply by the conditions in which they are asked to learn.

One of the impacts of poverty can be seen in achievement test score data (NCES, 2019). The number of free and reduced lunches is one indicator of poverty in a school. Table 18.3 compares the reading test scores of fourth and eighth grade students who were eligible to those not eligible for free and reduced lunches.

Table 18.3. Socioeconomic Status and Reading Test Scores

Year	Grade 4		Grade 8	
	not eligible	*eligible*	*not eligible*	*eligible*
2019	235	207	275	250
2017	236	208	277	253
2015	237	209	277	253
2013	236	207	278	254

Average reading scale score (out of a possible 500), correlated with the number of students eligible for free or reduced lunch from 2013–2019 (NCES, 2019).

Poverty and Stress

Acute stress is severe stress resulting from exposure to trauma such as abuse, violence, or death (Jensen, 2009). *Chronic stress* is exposure to high levels of stress sustained over time. It can adversely impact physical, emotional, and psychological functioning as well as cognitive functioning. This all impacts children's ability to learn.

Children living in poverty are subject to more stress than those not living in poverty (Ormrod et al., 2020). A *stressor* is anything that threatens to disrupt homeostasis. *Homeostasis* is the body's ability to achieve equilibrium, to bring it back to normal after it has experienced stress of some sort. Stressors for children living in poverty often include things such as toxins, exposure to violence, drug use, malnutrition, overcrowded living conditions, substandard housing, unsafe neighborhoods, divorce, financial strain, or loss of a family member. Stressors can also be psychological such as criticism, neglect, social exclusion, or constant failure and humiliation. These can all disrupt homeostasis, making it more difficult to achieve a normal state.

Stress triggers the body's fight-or-flight mechanism. Here the body reacts by pumping out an increased amount of the three stress hormones: adrenaline, cortisol, and norepinephrine. The body is well-equipped to handle short bits of stress; however, production of fight/flight stress hormones over time (chronic stress) can atrophy areas of the brain that control emotional regulation, empathy, and social functioning. Also, chronic stress over time challenges the body's ability to achieve homeostasis.

RESILIENCE

Students *at risk* are those who face obstacles and barriers to learning or completing their education. They are in danger of failing. Living in poverty is one of the factors that puts students at risk. *Resilience* is a person's capacity to recover quickly from difficulties. In an educational setting, resilience is a characteristic that enables some learners to rise above the obstacles and barriers to achieve success in school. Eggen and Kauchak (2013) describe four school practices that promote resilience:

1. **Teachers have high and uncompromising academic standards.** They expect all children can learn and will learn. They emphasize mastery of content and skills versus simply completing assignments or getting high test scores. This, however, is different from simply challenging students or setting unrealistic standards. Rather, teachers teach within the zone of proximal development and differentiate instruction in ways that enable all students to achieve their full potential.
2. **There are strong personal bonds between teachers and students.** Teachers interact frequently with students and get to know families and

communities. These are teachers who are not simply performing pedagogical tricks in front of students. Nor are they just trying to shape behaviors through rewards and punishments. Instead, these teachers see relationships as a prerequisite to teaching and learning.

3. **There is order and high structure in the school and classrooms.** Order and structure are different from manipulation and control. Structure is where the rules are visible and consistently enforced. As well, there are orderly procedures in place throughout the school and in classrooms. Students know what these are and why they are used.

4. **There is participation in after-school activities.** Sports, drama, the arts, and other types of clubs enable students to form positive connections with the school and with caring adults. Of course, to participate in these activities they must exist in the first place along with competent, caring adults in charge.

Chapter Nineteen

Disability and Race

A disability is not a disorder or deficit; rather, it is merely a difference, a slight variation on the common theme of humanity.

EDUCATION FOR ALL

Disability is an area that often intersects with race (*intersectionality*). This intersectionality is described in this chapter.

It Is a Social Construct

The Americans with Disabilities Act (ADA) defines *disability* as a physical or mental impairment that substantially limits one or more major life activities. Major life activities include, but are not limited to, "care for ones' self, performing manual tasks, seeing, hearing, eating, sleeping, walking, standing, lifting, bending, speaking, breathing, learning, reading, concentrating, thinking, communicating, and working." Like race (see Chapter 20), disability is a social construct based on the idea of a mythical norm or average (Shifrer et al., 2016). In other words, human beings designed disability constructs to categorize other human beings based on their idea of what they think a normal human being is or is supposed to be.

Models of Disabilities

Theoretical models provide structures for perceiving the world and thinking about things that exist in that world. Two common disability models are the medical model and the social model.

The medical model. The *medical model* views disability as something that is "wrong" with a person's body or mind. Here, the term "disorder" is often used in place of "disability." For example, in the *Diagnostic and Statistical Manual of Mental Disorders* (DSM-5), intellectual disabilities, autism spectrum disorder, attention deficit hyperactivity disorder, and specific learning disorder are all listed under *neurodevelopmental "disorders"* (APA, 2013). A disorder is the term used to indicate that some part of the body or mind is not functioning as it should. (There is an order that should be, and this thing is out of order.) Within the medical model, disabilities (or disorders) are viewed as deficits (Connor et al., 2019). Once diagnosed, people with disabilities are prescribed treatments to "fix" their disorders. Trained specialists administer the treatments in order to get the disabled person as close to "normal" as possible. Sadly, the medical model still dominates the special education system, a system in which students of color are disproportionately represented (Artiles, 2017; Connor, 2017; Fish, 2019; Shifrer et al., 2016; Voulgarides et al., 2017). This means that in our educational systems, a disproportionate number of students of color are seen as having a deficit.

The social model. In contrast to the medical model, *the social model* suggests that people with physical or other impairments are disabled by the way in which society acts (Fish, 2019). Here the disability lies not within the individual, but on the social plane. With this model, a distinction is made between an impairment and a disability. An *impairment* is a condition or a part of the body or mind that is nonstandard. For example, being blind, missing a limb, having a defective organ, or having a mental health condition are examples of having impairments. A *disability* is the disadvantages or restrictions caused by a social group that ignores people with impairments, thereby excluding them from full participation in the mainstream of that social group (Oliver, 1996). In other words, restrictions turn an impairment into a disability. No restriction, no disability. Restriction, disability.

In an educational setting, the following types of restrictions often turn impairments into disabilities: (a) class sizes that are too large, (b) poor quality of classroom instruction, (c) unqualified or underqualified teachers, (d) one-size-fits-all types of instruction or programs, (e) high-stakes testing, (f) mismatches between students' culture and classroom curriculum, (g) culturally biased assessment and instruction, (h) overly harsh and unjust discipline, (i) teacher bias, and (j) generally treating students like products moving down a conveyer belt and not like people. And these types of restrictions are much more likely to occur in schools serving poorer communities (Coutinho et al., 2002; USCCR, 2019), which (by the way) tend to include students of color at disproportionately higher rates (NCES, 2019).

Public Law 94-142

In 1975, Congress passed Public Law 94-142—Education of All Handi-capped Children Act. It was later amended and is now called the Individuals with Disabilities Education Act (IDEA). This law states that in order for schools to receive federal funds, they must provide free, appropriate public education (FAPE) to all children with disabilities. Further, these students must receive special education services in the least restrictive environment (LRE). This means that to the greatest extent possible, students with special needs are to be educated in a general education classroom.

Figure 19.1 contains a continuum of services for special needs students from most to least restrictive. When reviewing the literature on dispropor-tionality in special education, it becomes clear that both *appropriate* and *least restrictive* are subjective terms open to a variety of interpretations (Banks, 2017; Fish, 2019; Shifrer et al., 2016).

Appropriate. Appropriate education means that instruction is directly related to each students' individual educational needs. Yet, instruction in special education settings is too often more standardized than individualized. That is, whole-class instruction is used to implement standardized instruc-tional programs and methods (Allington, 2013; Denton et al., 2003; Swanson, 2008; Swanson & Vaughn, 2010). In terms of reading instruction, this can

Most restrictive	• *Home or institution.* Students are provided special education services at home, or they reside in a treatment center in which education is provided.
	• *Special school.* Students go to a special school designed to meet their needs.
	• *Full-time special classrooms.* Students attend a special education classroom full-time in a general education school. This allows them contact with general education peers only during nonacademic periods.
	• *Part-time in special classrooms.* Students reside in a special education classroom but are pulled for part of the day to attend some general education classes (often non-academic classes such as phy ed, art, music, etc.).
	• *Part-time in general education classrooms.* Students reside in a general education classroom but are pulled for part of the day to attend specific programs in a special education resource room.
Least restrictive	• *General Education with consultation.* Students attend full time in a general education classroom. Educational specialists consult with the general education teacher to design instruction to meet their needs.

Figure 19.1. A continuum of services for students with special needs.

often have a deleterious effect (Allington, 2013; Bentum & Aaron, 2003). There are no magical one-size-fits-all programs that work best for all students (Allington & McGill-Franzen, 2017). There are no super-secret special education strategies that only specially trained special education teachers can implement (Johnson, 2020). Instead, there are master teachers who have a variety of research-based tools in their teaching toolbox. And these tools should always be adopted and adapted to meet the unique needs of their students. In other words, instruction should always be modified so that it is appropriate to meet the needs of the student and teaching situation. What might be appropriate for a third-grade student with reading difficulties in Blackwater, Arizona, is most likely not appropriate for a third-grade student with reading difficulties in Edina, Minnesota.

Least restrictive. The least restrictive environment means that students with special learning needs should be in the general education classroom to the greatest extent possible. Special education should be a service, not a place. However, when compared to white students with the same disability label, African American students are more often educated in these highly restrictive, segregated special education settings (Annamma et al., 2013; Banks, 2017; Blanchett, 2006; Connor, 2017; Shifrer et al., 2016; Zhang et al., 2014). And once students are placed in a segregated program, the chances that they will drop out of school, be arrested, be imprisoned, and/or be unemployed after graduating all increase (Harry & Klinger, 2014; Peterson & Hittie, 2010; USCCR, 2019). It is impossible to deny the fact that, whether intended or unintended, there are systems in place that disadvantage and restrict people of color. This is called systemic racism (see Chapter 20). This is prevalent in the special education system.

SEGREGATION AND INCLUSION

Both segregated and inclusive classrooms are used to meet the learning needs of students identified as having a disability. Each of these is examined here.

Segregated Classrooms

Segregated instruction is any instruction that occurs outside the general education classroom. Segregated instruction could include full-time placement in a special education classroom (see Figure 19.1). It could also involve some sort of pull-out services where students are pulled out of the general education classroom for "specialized" instruction for part of the day or for single subject areas. This usually takes place in a special education resource room.

Diminished educational outcomes. At one time it was thought that smaller class sizes and additional adult resources found in a segregated special education classroom would enable teachers to provide individualized instruction that would meet the special needs of each student. It was thought as well that this would lead to improved learning outcomes for these students. This is not the case. It turns out that educational outcomes are more often diminished rather than enhanced in segregated settings (Allington & McGill-Franzen, 2017; Artiles, 2017; Connor, 2017; Peterson & Hittie, 2010). This is because students in segregated special education settings frequently do not receive the same quality of education as students in general education classrooms (Banks, 2017; Benner et al., 2011; Harry & Klingner, 2014; Voulgarides & Tefera, 2017). Also, the instruction here often is neither individualized nor appropriate (Allington & McGill-Franzen, 2017; Zhang & Katsiyannis, 2020).

Reading instruction. To illustrate, we will examine reading instruction. Within the special education system, approximately 85% of all the students receive some sort of "specialized" reading instruction (Sayeski et al., 2015). The problem, however, is that students within this system rarely experience accelerated reading (Allington, 2011; Allington & McGill-Franzen, 2017; Denton et al., 2003; Moody et al., 2000). This may be because they rarely get improved access to expert reading instruction (Allington, 2013; Harry & Klingner, 2014). Students in special education resource rooms are taught by special education teachers, not reading specialists.

A special education teacher is not a reading specialist (Allington, 1994). The general orientation and the initial teacher preparation requirements are much different (Benner et al., 2011; Brownell et al., 2010; Brownell et al., 2005). These differences are reflected in the number and types of standards required by national accreditation organizations. For example, significantly fewer standards related to literacy instruction are required for preservice special education teachers than for preservice elementary education teachers (CAEP, 2018; CEC 2020). As well, the standards required by the Council for Exceptional Children (CEC) for special education teachers focus on assessment, data collection, behavior management, and direct instruction. There are no required CEC standards that focus specifically on developing students' ability to create meaning with print.

As a result, the "specialized" reading instruction provided in special education settings is too often a one-size-fits-all program or method that relies primarily on direct instruction of low-level reading subskills (Denton et al., 2003; Eppley & Dudley-Marling, 2018; Klingner et al., 2010). While direct instruction is effective for learning low-level skills, it is extremely ineffective for developing high-level thinking, understanding complex concepts, and acquiring sophisticated skills (Allington, 2013). And when direct instruction is overused to teach low-level reading subskills, students have few (if any) opportunities to read good books, engage in social interaction around good books, or develop complex thinking. In other words, if only low-level skills are taught in special education classrooms, only low-level learning occurs.

Inclusive Classrooms

In an inclusive classroom, instruction for students with special learning needs occurs within the general education classroom setting. Here, the teacher differentiates a common curriculum to meet the special learning needs of all students. Peterson and Hittie (2010) found that, when compared to students in segregated settings, students in inclusive classrooms encounter (a) greater academic expectations, (b) a richer learning environment, (c) more effective teaching strategies, and (d) more exposure to modeling by more-able peers, all of which enhance learning. Also, in inclusive classroom settings the social and emotional outcomes are better and there is greater achievement of individualized education program (IEP) goals (Freeman & Alkin, 2000).

Multilevel strategies. But simply putting students with special learning needs in a general education classroom does not make it an inclusive classroom. Also, just putting a special education teacher in the general education classroom as a co-teacher also does not make it an inclusive classroom. Instead, inclusive classrooms are those in which the classroom teachers have the knowledge and skills necessary to make inclusive teaching successful. They have a variety of multilevel strategies for differentiating a common curriculum. These could include some or all of the following: universal design for learning (UDL), contract learning, tiered assignments, workshop approaches for reading and writing, learning centers, goal setting, curriculum compacting, flexible grouping, workstations, jigsawing, project-based learning, interest groups, shared reading, close reading, and menus.

Effective inclusive classrooms. There are three elements necessary for effective inclusive classrooms: The first element is having an optimal number of students in the classroom. This number varies; however, preschool through grade 1 should generally have a maximum of 12 to 15 students, and grades 2 and above, a maximum of 20 students. Smaller class sizes enable the special learning needs of more students to be addressed within the inclusive general education classroom.

The second element necessary for effective inclusive classrooms is knowledgeable and skilled teachers. This means there must be continued professional development opportunities for teachers. The goal here would be to enhance teachers' knowledge of and ability to use a variety of multilevel teaching strategies (see above).

The third element for effective inclusive classrooms is time to adequately plan, have conversations with other teachers, reflect, and revise. Some believe that effective teaching is simply a matter of buying the right program or product, taking it out of the box, reading the instructions, and then implementing it with fidelity. However, students are not standardized products. Communities, schools, classrooms, and teachers are not all the same. Every pedagogical strategy, program, method, or curriculum needs to be adopted and adapted to meet the unique learning needs of real-life students. This all takes planning and time.

DISPROPORTIONALITY

There is a disproportionate number of students of color within the special education system (Blanchet, 2006; USCCR, 2019; Zhang & Katsiyannis, 2020). Disproportionality is most present in the three high-incidence categories: learning disabilities, emotional/behavioral disorders, and intellectual disabilities (Artiles, 2017). These categories also tend to have the most stigma attached to them (Fish, 2019). They are also the most subjective categories. Here, a teacher referral is a necessary part of the identification process. Teacher bias related to what is "normal" is one of the factors that leads to this disproportionality (Connor, 2017; Fish, 2019). In fact, varying forms of bias and subjectivity exist in all parts of the process used to determine students' eligibility for special education services, including teacher referral, testing, and team meetings (Fish, 2019).

Within the larger educational system, there are also disproportionate numbers of students of color involved in disciplinary actions, suspensions, school dropout rates, involvement with the legal system, and poverty (USCCR, 2019). This disproportionality correlates with other aspects of society such as poverty, poor housing, low-level and low-paying jobs, unemployment, insufficient health care, single-parent households, and rates of incarceration (Conner, 2017; Zhang & Katsiyannis, 2020). These are just some of the variables that serve to disadvantage and restrict people of color. This is also an example of structural racism:

> We use the term structural racism to define the many factors that contribute to and facilitate the maintenance of racial inequities in the United States today. A structural racism analytical framework identifies aspects of our history and

culture that have allowed the privileges associated with "whiteness" and the disadvantages associated with "color" to endure and adapt over time. It points out the ways in which public policies and institutional practices contribute to inequitable racial outcomes. It lays out assumptions and stereotypes that are embedded in our culture that, in effect, legitimize racial disparities, and it illuminates the ways in which progress toward racial equity is undermined. (Fulbright-Anderson et al., 2005, p. 2)

SPECIFIC LEARNING DISABILITY

As stated above, "disability" is a social construct. A "learning disability" is an educational construct. A *learning disability* is said to exist when there is a discrepancy between a student's expected ability and his or her achievement in one of seven areas: basic reading skill, reading comprehension, listening comprehension, oral expression, written expression, math calculation, and mathematics reasoning. The U.S. Department of Education's definition is in Textbox 19.1 (USDE, 2018).

TEXTBOX 19.1. U.S. DEPARTMENT OF EDUCATION DEFINITION OF SPECIFIC LEARNING DISABILITY

IN GENERAL: The term "specific learning disability" means a disorder in one or more of the basic psychological processes involved in understanding or in using language, spoken or written, which disorder may manifest itself in imperfect ability to listen, think, speak, read, write, spell, or do mathematical calculations.

SPECIFIC LEARNING DISABILITY: "Specific learning disability" means a condition within the pupil affecting learning, relative to potential, and is manifested by interference with the acquisition, organization, storage, retrieval, manipulation, or expression of information so that the pupil does not learn at an adequate rate when provided with the usual developmental opportunities and instruction from a regular school environment.

Using the medical model, The DSM-5 uses the term "disorder" vs. "disability" to define a specific learning disorder (see Textbox 19.2) (APA, 2013):

TEXTBOX 19.2. DSM-5 DEFINITION OF
SPECIFIC LEARNING DISORDER

Difficulties learning and using academic skills, as indicated by the presence of at least one of the following symptoms that have persisted for at least 6 months, despite the provision of interventions that target those difficulties:

1. Inaccurate or slow and effortful word reading.
2. Difficulty understanding the meaning of what is read.
3. Difficulties with written expression.
4. Difficulties mastering number sense, number facts, or calculation.
5. Difficulties with mathematical reasoning.

Please consider this: learning is a natural human condition. Humans do it from the day they are born until they die. Thus, the term "learning disability" has meaning only in the artificial confines of a school environment. However, humans eventually leave the school petri dish and enter the real world. Thus, schools must be very careful to not define any student's potential by giving him or her a label such as "learning disability" when in fact, sometimes what is called a "learning disability" might actually be one of the following:

1. a learning-certain-kinds-of-things disability,
2. a learning-school-things disability,
3. a learning-things-you-don't-want-to-learn disability,
4. a learning unnaturally disability,
5. a learning-not-as-fast-as-you-think-students-should-learn disability,
6. a teaching disability,
7. an educational-system disability,
8. a bad-things-happening-at-home disability, or
9. an over-crowded-classroom disability.

EMOTIONAL OR BEHAVIORAL DISORDERS

An emotional or behavioral disorder (EBD) might be said to exist when one's emotions or behaviors get in the way of learning and participating in the learning environment. The U.S. Department of Education's definition is in Textbox 19.3.

TEXTBOX 19.3. U.S. DEPARTMENT OF EDUCATION DEFINITION OF EMOTIONAL OR BEHAVIORAL DISORDERS

Emotional or behavioral disorders means an established pattern of one or more of the following emotional or behavioral responses: (a) withdrawal or anxiety, depression, problems with mood, or feelings of self worth; (b) disordered thought processes with unusual behavior patterns and atypical communication styles; or (c) aggression, hyperactivity, or impulsivity.

The established pattern of emotional or behavioral responses must adversely affect educational or developmental performance, including intrapersonal, academic, vocational, or social skills; be significantly different from appropriate age, cultural, or ethnic norms; and be more than temporary, expected responses to stressful events in the environment. The emotional or behavioral responses must be consistently exhibited in at least three different settings, two of which must be educational settings, and one other setting in either the home, child care, or community. The responses must not be primarily the result of intellectual, sensory, or acute or chronic physical health conditions.

This high-incidence disability category is also subjected to teacher bias and cultural norms for the initial referral for special education placement. However, many behavior "disorders" can be undiagnosed mental health conditions, or they might be students' natural reactions to adverse conditions. Also the special education system seems to be designed to deal only with the "B" in EBD, not the "E." That is, it addresses behaviors rather than the cause of behaviors. If teachers are emotionally present and attuned to the social, emotional, physical, and safety needs of all their students, many of the problem behaviors do not appear. Finally smaller class sizes enable teachers to better help students through difficult times.

INTELLECTUAL DISABILITY

As stated above, a disability is not a deficit or deficiency; rather, it is a variation on the human theme. The official definitions for an intellectual disability are in Textboxes 19.4 and 19.5 below.

TEXTBOX 19.4. U.S. DEPARTMENT OF EDUCATION DEFINITION OF INTELLECTUAL DISABILITY

Intellectual disability means significantly subaverage general intellectual functioning, existing concurrently with deficits in adaptive behavior and manifested during the developmental period, that adversely affects a child's educational performance. The term "intellectual disability" was formerly termed "mental retardation."

TEXTBOX 19.5. DSM-5 DEFINITION OF INTELLECTUAL DISABILITY

Intellectual disability (intellectual developmental disorder) is a disorder with onset during the developmental period that includes both intellectual and adaptive functioning deficits in conceptual, social, and practice domains.

ATTENTION DEFICIT HYPERACTIVITY DISORDER

Students with Attention Deficit Hyperactivity Disorder (ADHD) have a hard time concentrating or focusing. The U.S. Department of Education defers to the DSM-5 when offering a medical-based definition. It is "a persistent pattern of inattention and/or hyperactivity-impulsivity that interferes with function or development" (APA 2013, p. 31). The "symptoms" include the following:

Inattention: Six or more symptoms of inattention for children up to age 16 years, or five or more for adolescents age 17 years and older and adults; symptoms of inattention have been present for at least 6 months, and they are inappropriate for developmental level:

- Often fails to give close attention to details or makes careless mistakes in schoolwork, at work, or with other activities.
- Often has trouble holding attention on tasks or play activities.
- Often does not seem to listen when spoken to directly.
- Often does not follow through on instructions and fails to finish schoolwork, chores, or duties in the workplace (e.g., loses focus, side-tracked).
- Often has trouble organizing tasks and activities.

- Often avoids, dislikes, or is reluctant to do tasks that require mental effort over a long period of time (such as schoolwork or homework).
- Often loses things necessary for tasks and activities (e.g. school materials, pencils, books, tools, wallets, keys, paperwork, eyeglasses, mobile telephones).
- Is often easily distracted
- Is often forgetful in daily activities (APA, 2013, p. 32)

Hyperactivity and Impulsivity: Six or more symptoms of hyperactivity-impulsivity for children up to age 16 years, or five or more for adolescents age 17 years and older and adults; symptoms of hyperactivity-impulsivity have been present for at least 6 months to an extent that is disruptive and inappropriate for the person's developmental level:

- Often fidgets with or taps hands or feet, or squirms in seat.
- Often leaves seat in situations when remaining seated is expected.
- Often runs about or climbs in situations where it is not appropriate (adolescents or adults may be limited to feeling restless).
- Often unable to play or take part in leisure activities quietly.
- Is often "on the go" acting as if "driven by a motor."
- Often talks excessively.
- Often blurts out an answer before a question has been completed.
- Often has trouble waiting their turn.
- Often interrupts or intrudes on others (e.g., butts into conversations or games) (APA, 2013, pp. 32–33)

There are two things to consider here. First, these criteria are all based on a subjective determination of "normal." This serves to reify parochial conceptions of normality and abnormality where teacher bias plays a large part in the initial referral. Second, these "symptoms" are also common effects of poor nutrition, poverty, and chronic and acute stress, all of which disproportionately affect minority students.

OTHER

In this chapter, four disability categories were briefly described. The U.S. Department of Education recognizes 13 disability categories:

- autism
- deaf-blindness
- deafness
- emotional disturbance

- hearing impairment
- intellectual disability
- multiple disabilities
- orthopedic impairment
- other health impairment (including ADHD)
- specific learning disability
- speech or language impairment
- traumatic brain injury
- visual impairment (including blindness)

BIG IDEAS

1. Disability and race are both social constructs.
2. A disability is not a disorder or deficit; rather, it is merely a difference.
3. The medical model views a disability as a disorder within the individual.
4. The social model views disability as a restriction or disadvantage imposed on people with impairments that restricts them from fully participating in society.
5. Inclusive classrooms are generally more effective than segregated instruction for students with special needs if taught by a knowledgeable and skilled teacher with class sizes that enable multilevel instruction.
6. There are a disproportionate number of students of color in the special education system.

Chapter Twenty

Systemic Racism and Critical Race Theory

This chapter examines systemic racism and critical race theory.

SYSTEMIC RACISM

Systemic racism is that which serves to disadvantage and restrict people of color in ways that advance the interests of those in power (who, by the way, are overwhelming white males). Whether implicit or explicit, intended or unintended, white racism creates and maintains a racial hierarchy that provides advantage to the white majority in terms of opportunities and resources (Kohli et al., 2019). Specifically, there is a finger on the scale to ensure that the dominant class has continued access to better jobs, loans, housing, schools, teachers, and health care, and that they are treated differently by the criminal justice system.

The Apple Theory

Systemic racism must be differentiated from racist acts. A racist act involves one or more persons engaged in discrimination, bigotry, hatred, violence, or pejoration that is directed against one or more individuals and is based on race. While racist acts are a result of racism, a myopic conception of racism deflects responsibility and diminishes the full understanding of racism (Blanchett, 2006). Some insist that racism is simply the actions of "a few bad apples." This is what those in power would have us believe, that racism is just a few bad apples here and there. According to this apple theory, ending racism is simply a matter of apple hunting. But the apple theory ignores and serves to cover up the larger systematic suppression and oppression of minority populations used by those with economic and political power to maintain that power.

A System

Racism exists within the context of a societal system. A system is an interacting and interdependent set of elements that influence each other and work together to form a unified ever-evolving whole. The whole is contained within each part, and each part is contained within the whole. According to systems theory, anything happening to one part of the system affects the whole. Included within our societal system are a variety of subsystems, each of which has been infected by the racism virus. These include legal systems, prison systems, economic systems, political systems, and educational systems. Racism is like a bit of poison in the water tank. You cannot drink a single cup and expect it not to be tainted.

Cultural Superiority and a Mythical Norm

Systemic racism also takes the form of cultural superiority. Here, the values and customs of the majority culture are used by the majority culture as the standard to which all others are compared. Right and wrong, good and bad, normal and abnormal are all determined by how closely actions, entities, and experiences align with those of the majority culture (which in most cases is white, middle-class, Eurocentric, and largely Christian). People, groups, values, views, behaviors, and practices that are not reflective of this mythical norm are seen as deficient or deviant. In other words, there is a standardized way that things should be. The parochial assumption is that "they" should be like "us." "If only they were like us, all their problems would go away. If they would just assimilate, everything would be just right."

CRITICAL RACE THEORY

A theory is a way to explain a set of facts. It explains phenomena by connecting the data-dots to form a picture. Different theories connect different data dots differently. Critical race theory (CRT) is one such theory used to explain and understand the phenomenon known as systemic racism. CRT invites us to critically examine our policies, practices, assessment, curriculum, courses, pedagogy, and traditions. The questions in Textbox 20.1 can be used toward this end.

TEXTBOX 20.1. QUESTIONS RELATED TO CRT

1. Who gains? Who is exploited?
2. Who gets the resources? Who is deprived?
3. Who is advantaged? Who is disadvantaged?
4. How are marginalized populations depicted and portrayed?
5. Whose voice dominates and whose is silenced?
6. Who is included? Who is excluded?
7. Who gets opportunities? Who does not?
8. Who gets punished? Who gets rewarded?
9. Who gets attention? Who gets ignored?
10. Who is making money? Who is paying money?
11. What makes it difficult for some and easier for others?
12. Which communities get the well-paying jobs? Which don't?

Seven Big Ideas

Described here are seven big ideas common to most understandings of CRT:

1. Racism is normal. It is so ingrained in our societal consciousness that most do not see it; however, our brains see racism in the form of implicit bias (Abiodun, 2019; Bell, 1992; Cunningham et al., 2004; Eberhardt, 2005; Liberman et al., 2005; Ronquillo et al., 2007; Sankar et al., 2018; Stanley et al., 2008). As well, our policies, programs, laws, and procedures do (Brooks-Immel & Murray, 2017; Linley, 2018). This is systemic racism. And it exists, unseen within most societal systems. For change to occur, we must expose systemic racism as well as that which maintains and perpetuates it. Toward this end, the questions in Textbox 20.1 can be used to critically examine all aspects of our societal system.

2. Change occurs only when it aligns with the interests of those in power (Bell, 1992; Brown & Jackson, 2013; Delgado & Stefancic, 2017). In other words, advances for people of color will occur only when it coincides with changing economic conditions and the self-interests of elite whites. The current protests will only be successful when they hit the pocketbooks of those in power or when they threaten the political power of those in power. Within each system, the hard questions to ask is: Who stands to gain in the current system? More simply, who is making money? Who is getting resources?

3. Race is a social construct (Annamma et al., 2016; Delgado & Stefancic, 2017; Ladson-Billings, 2016. It has no basis in biology. Race is an arbitrary category based on physical appearance that society has created based around the idea of a mythical white norm. These arbitrary categories become used as a sorting mechanism. This sorting has both material and psychological impacts, creating winners and losers.

4. No person has a single identity (Delgado & Stefancic, 2017). Instead, race intersects with gender, social class, ability, sexual identity, and other areas of marginalization. This creates an interaction in which collectively or in combination they exert a more powerful influence than they do individually.

5. All people in a category do not think and act the same (Ladson-Billings, 2016). Physical characteristics referred to by racial terms are not indicative of deeper, underlying commonalities or shared traits. This is the idea of non-essentialism. One famous black person does not speak for all black people. One person of color should not be asked to be the spokesperson to try to explain systemic racism.

6. The stories of people must be heard (Ladson-Billings, 2016; Linley, 2018; Taylor, 2016). Hearing and honoring the perceptions and experiences of real people is essential in making progress toward social justice and racial equity. However, in education, peoples' voices are muted in two significant ways. The first occurs through the overreliance on controlled experimental research studies to establish cause-effect relationships. The federal government has determined that this type of research (known as the "gold standard") is the only legitimate way of knowing, thereby delegitimizing other forms of scholarship (Johnson, 2021). The result is a distorted picture of the very reality it seeks to portray. For example, a controlled experimental study may demonstrate that a certain practice is effective, but it does not tell you for whom, how, under what circumstances, for what purpose, for how long, and to what degree.

This points to the importance of recognizing qualitative research as a legitimate and valued form of knowing as well as controlled experimental studies. Types of qualitative research include surveys, interviews, observations, ethnographies, grounded theory research, case studies, and historical research methods. These should all be used to fully understand human phenomena. All quantitative data must be considered in their broader contexts.

The second way of disallowing the voices of marginalized groups in education is through the disremembering and misremembering of history. Here, history is described only through the lens of the privileged majority. The histories of marginalized groups are misremembered using cartoonish configurations, distortions, omissions, and blatant misrepresentations. Books that illustrate a more complete remembering include *An African American and Latinx History of the United States* (Ortiz, 2018), *An Indigenous Peoples' History of the United States* (Dunbar-Ortiz, 2014), and *Caste: The Origins of Our Discontents,* (Wilkerson, 2020). Books like these describe a decidedly different version of U.S. history than the McGraw-Hill version of reality provided in most K–12 curriculums. Here, the atrocities of slavery, the greed of colonization, the avarice of imperialism, and the wanton genocide of indigenous peoples are fully portrayed.

7. Cultural parochialism and white superiority are factors in maintaining systemic racism (Ansley, 1997; Gillborn, 2013). A belief that one's own culture is the correct one to be used as a standard of comparison is called cultural parochialism. Here, practices, customs, lifestyles, traditions, views, and values that do not align with the dominant white culture are deemed to be defective, deviant, or inferior. Thus, right and wrong, good and bad, normal and abnormal are all determined by the majority white culture. This is white superiority. This last idea must be considered as a factor contributing to the perpetuation of systemic racism in teacher preparation programs.

Chapter Twenty-One

Culturally Responsive Teaching

Culturally responsive teaching is "a set of practices designed to build on students' cultural and linguistic backgrounds as teaching and learning occur" (Cruz et al., 2010, p. 43).

THREE INTERCONNECTED ELEMENTS

Gloria Ladson-Billings (2014) describes culturally responsive teaching as consisting of three interacting and interconnected elements: (a) high academic standards that focus on students' total intellectual growth, (b) cultural competence and inclusion, and (c) critical or sociopolitical consciousness. None of these by themselves can be said to be culturally response teaching. It is the interaction of these three that creates culturally responsive teaching (see Figure 21.1). However, this framework enables us to move forward in our understanding of CRT. Each of these elements is described below.

Total Intellectual Growth

Culturally responsive teaching includes high academic standards that focus on developing students' total intellectual growth. Three components of this are described here:

- **Solving problems and creating products.** Learning is seen as the intellectual growth that students experience as a result of classroom instruction and other learning experiences (Ladson-Billings, 2017). However, intellectual growth is not confined to scores on a standardized test. Instead, total intellectual growth includes enhanced capability in the use of problem-solving,

Culturally Responsive Teaching

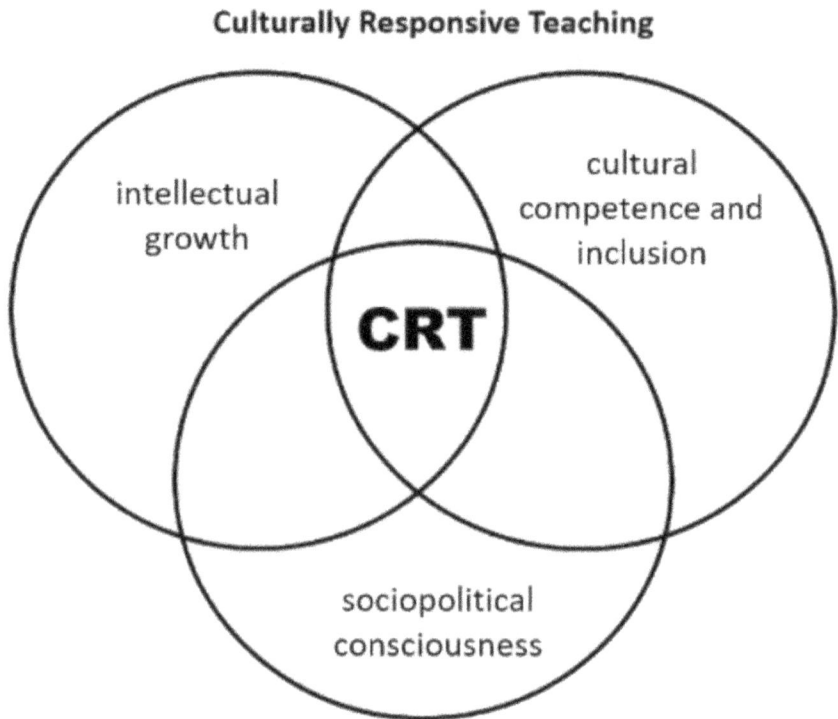

intellectual growth

cultural competence and inclusion

CRT

sociopolitical consciousness

Figure 21.1.   Culturally responsive teaching.

critical and creative thinking, moral reasoning, and communication skills all of which are used to address real-life situations. In other words, it is an improvement of one's ability to solve problems and create products that are of value in one or more cultural settings. This, by the way, is how Howard Gardner defines intelligence (Gardner, 1999).

• **Transformation.** Yes, academic achievement as traditionally measured on standardized tests is still important; however, it is seen as a means to a greater end. The greater end here is real-life problem-solving used to achieve transformation on personal, environmental, and social levels (Banks, 2002; Hammond, 2015). Toward this end, culturally responsive teaching includes teaching some of the following skills: problem-solving skills, critical and creative thinking skills, written and oral communication skills, and social and interpersonal skills. It also includes some of the following types of teaching strategies: experiential learning, cooperative learning, discovery learning, inquiry learning, problem-based learning, contract learning, and service learning.

- **Self-actualization.** Finally, full intellectual growth includes the ability to recognize, embrace, and utilize all dimensions of oneself. This is a form of self-actualization, the term used to describe the natural unfolding and realization of one's full potential (see Chapter 5). Thus social, interpersonal, emotional-intrapersonal, and physical dimensions are all addressed. However, these all take place within the context of cultural competence and inclusion (see below).

Cultural Competence and Inclusion

There are four parts to this element.

The teacher has an interest in students' cultures and lived experiences. While it is not possible to have in-depth knowledge of all the cultures that students bring to the classroom or to completely understand all students' lived experiences, it is possible to take an interest and to learn. This is of course predicated on trust and relationships with the teacher and with the other students in the class (Hammond, 2015). It also means that there must be outreach and interaction between the teacher and community at some level. Simply put, the teacher has to get out and talk with people within the community. As well, the teacher should also try to learn about and understand the art, music, and writings that speak to students.

Students' culture is used as a basis for learning. Students learn more and learn more easily when new knowledge is connected to old knowledge (Johnson, 2019). Thus, as stated above, culturally responsive teachers invite students to bring their cultures, histories, experiences, values, art, music, and ways of seeing the world into the classroom. These are used as the basis for students' new learning (Hammond, 2015). In this way, the curriculum and classroom instruction have some resemblance to the community from which the learners come (Gay, 2018).

Multiple communication styles are included. CRT helps students understand and navigate cultural norms for communication. Rather than trying to negate or suppress students' current ways of communicating, they are taught how and when to code switch—that is, when it is and is not appropriate to use the various types of language and writing styles (Irizarry, 2017). Students are taught to appreciate their own ways of communicating while also learning to develop fluency in another. Ladson-Billings refers to the dominant academic language (DAL) as the culture of commerce and social advancement (2017). CRT does not diminish the language styles germane to any culture. Instead, it seeks to broaden students' cultural repertoire. It also recognizes that being bilingual, trilingual, or multilingual is far from being deficient; rather, it enhances students' ability to interact, succeed, and become agents of change in a global community (Lee & Walsh, 2017).

The historical context of systemic racism is recognized and included. Cultural understanding of any group cannot be separated from its historical context (Lee & Walsh, 2017). This calls for teachers to know a bit of history. Toward this end, three powerful and well-written books are recommended as a starting place: *An African American and Latinx History of the United States* by Paul Ortiz (2018), *Caste: The Origins of Our Discontents* by Isabel Wilkerson (2020), and *An Indigenous Peoples' History of the United States* by Roxanne Dunbar-Ortiz (2014). Older history books include *The Autobiography of Malcom X* by Malcom X and Alex Haley (1965), *The Fire Next Time* by James Baldwin (1991) and *Faces at the Bottom of the Well: The Permanence of Racism* by Derrick Bell (1992). These books can be used as assigned reading at the upper high school levels. They can also be used to inform curriculum for students in grades 1 and above. But most importantly, they provide teachers with some of the historical perspective necessary to understand students' cultures.

Support Students' Critical Consciousness

It critically examines existing frameworks and practices. CRT includes learning experiences that invite students to critically examine established ways of thinking, seeing, and knowing. This means examining and evaluating curricula, books, policies, practices, and culture through a racial equity and social justice lens (Lee & Walsh, 2017). This also means that students must be given the tools to address social, cultural, economic, and political problems. In this way, students are able to become agents of change in addressing social justice and racial equity issues. These things are all aligned with the basic aims of critical race theory (Delgado & Stefancic, 2017; Ladson-Billings, 2016)

It is reflective. CRT invites students to identify, examine, and clarify their own values (Johnson, 2009). This is much more powerful and lasting than simply telling students what they should value or how they should behave. Values clarification activities usually involve defining, listing, ranking, or rating things that students' find important to them (see Appendix B). These activities come in many different forms, but they should have some or all of the following four characteristics: First, students' insights and ideas are respected. Teachers do not correct, evaluate, or validate students' responses. Second, students are free to make choices. Teachers do not lead students toward a predetermined choice or response. Third, there is a discussion or sharing of ideas either before or after the activity. And fourth, students are encouraged to consider both the positive and negative consequences of their choices.

It is empowering. CRT empowers students by offering choices about what they learn, how they learn, and how they demonstrate their learning. This reflects a student-centered approach to teaching (Johnson, 2017). It is movement away from authoritarian, top-down relationships based on power and authority, toward more equal relationships based on principles of respect and a shared set of values. Instead of using power to control students in the school or classroom, relationships are used to invite students to cooperate in creating an effective learning environment and meaningful learning experiences.

It is emancipatory. CRT strives to liberate the mind from traditional ways of thinking, which tend to reflect a white, Eurocentric perspective (Freire, 1993; Gay, 2018). It invites students to untether themselves from the mainstream canons of knowledge and conventional ways of knowing in order to think about new things in new ways.

It incorporates real-life experiences. CRT seeks to bring students' real-life experiences into the classroom (Ladson-Billings, 2017). Instead of studying an abstract, academic world defined by a white, Eurocentric cultural perspective, learning is linked to students' lives to the greatest extent possible. The issues and problems germane to students are incorporated into the curriculum. Strategies like experiential learning, service learning, and problem-based learning are used to make real-world problems, experiences, and situations the basis of students' learning.

TWO BIG IDEAS

First, one of the major tenets of culturally responsive teaching is that students' current cultures are used as a necessary starting point for learning. Students are not expected to act white or to leave their cultures at the door. Instead, students' linguistic tools, their ways of seeing and being, and their background knowledge are used as a foundation for learning.

Second, culturally responsive teaching consists of three interconnected elements: (a) high academic standards that focus on students' total intellectual growth, (b) cultural competence and inclusion, and (c) critical or sociopolitical consciousness. These elements are interdependent, meaning that any individual element is not sufficient in and of itself. Instead, culturally responsive teaching is found at the intersection and interconnection of all three.

Chapter Twenty-Two

Mental Health for Children and Adolescents

This chapter will focus on the most common mental health disorders that occur in children and adolescents: mood disorders, anxiety disorders, eating disorders, schizophrenia, substance use disorder, and youth suicide (Evens et al., 2005). It ends with an examination of ways to promote mental health. The information here is not designed to enable you to make diagnoses; rather, the goal is to raise your level of awareness so that you might be able to inform parents and involve the appropriate mental health professionals when there are concerns.

ORDER AND DISORDER

One in five students ages 9–17 have experienced a mental health issue at some time (Auger, 2011). As well, there are large numbers who remain undiagnosed or who are diagnosed but left untreated. For these children and adolescents, mental health disorders can result in increased pain and suffering in their daily life and decreased school performance. Mental disorders can also limit their ability to achieve their full potential in all areas. However, a disorder assumes there is an order or some sort of norm. So, what is normal thinking and behaving? Much of what we think of as "normal" is culturally defined and situation-specific. In other words, what is normal in one culture or society may be abnormal in another. What is appropriate in one time and place is inappropriate in another. So, in describing mental disorders or psychology abnormalities, keep in mind that categories and labels are always a bit subjective.

Identify Adolescents with Mental Disorders

There are two things to keep in mind when thinking about mental disorders and adolescents: First, adolescence is a time of transition and turmoil as adolescents adapt to the significant changes in hormones, brain and physical development, emotions, cognition, behaviors, and interpersonal and social relationships. It is the beginning of sexual maturation, as well as a time of identifying values, personal identity, and future goals. It would be abnormal NOT to be a little abnormal during this time. Thus, you cannot look at adolescents the same way as adults when you consider mental health symptoms and criteria.

Second, identification is often difficult because most adolescents and young adults do not know what normal is. Since their own state of consciousness is all they have ever known or have access to, they have no sense of comparison. Education related to mental health helps adolescent students recognize some of the signs of a mental health disorder.

The National Institute of Mental Health (NIMH, 2021) lists the early warning signs for a mental disorder for young children in Textbox 22.1 and older children and adolescents in Textbox 22.2. Again, remember that many children and adolescents may display these behaviors from time to time. When deciding whether or not you should share a concern with parents, you must consider (a) the frequency of the symptoms, (b) the duration of the symptoms, and (c) the intensity of the symptoms.

TEXTBOX 22.1. EARLY WARNING SIGNS FOR YOUNG CHILDREN

- Have frequent tantrums or are intensely irritable much of the time
- Often talk about fears or worries
- Complain about frequent stomachaches or headaches with no known medical cause
- Are in constant motion and cannot sit quietly (*except* when they are watching videos or playing video games)
- Sleep too much or too little, have frequent nightmares, or seem sleepy during the day
- Are not interested in playing with other children or have difficulty making friends
- Struggle academically or have experienced a recent decline in grades
- Repeat actions or check things many times out of fear that something bad may happen

TEXTBOX 22.2. EARLY WARNING SIGNS FOR OLDER CHILDREN AND ADOLESCENTS

- Have lost interest in things that they used to enjoy
- Have low energy
- Sleep too much or too little, or seem sleepy throughout the day
- Are spending more and more time alone, and avoid social activities with friends or family
- Diet or exercise excessively, or fear gaining weight
- Engage in self-harm behaviors (such as cutting or burning their skin)
- Smoke, drink alcohol, or use drugs
- Engage in risky or destructive behavior alone or with friends
- Have thoughts of suicide
- Have periods of highly elevated energy and activity, and require much less sleep than usual
- Say that they think someone is trying to control their mind or that they hear things that other people cannot hear

MOOD DISORDERS

A mood disorder, sometimes call an affect disorder, is an emotional disturbance such as severe depression (major depressive disorder) or depression alternating with mania (bipolar disorder).

Major Depressive Disorder

As alluded to above, because of the often turbulent nature and natural mood swings of adolescents, this can be somewhat difficult to diagnose. Depression is an overwhelming sadness that lasts for a long time. You cannot just snap out of it. Textbox 22.3 describes common signs and symptoms of depression for children and teens (NIMH, 2021).

TEXTBOX 22.3. COMMON SIGNS AND SYMPTOMS OF DEPRESSION

- Persistent sad, anxious, or "empty" mood
- Feelings of hopelessness or pessimism
- Feelings of irritability, frustration, or restlessness
- Feelings of guilt, worthlessness, or helplessness

- Loss of interest or pleasure in hobbies or activities
- Decreased energy, fatigue, or being "slowed down"
- Difficulty concentrating, remembering, or making decisions
- Difficulty sleeping, early morning awakening, or oversleeping
- Changes in appetite or unplanned weight changes
- Aches or pains, headaches, cramps, or digestive problems without a clear physical cause and that do not ease even with treatment
- Suicide attempts or thoughts of death or suicide

The first onset of a major depressive disorder is often in adolescence (Evans et al., 2005). About 21% of females and 13% of males have experienced major depression at some time in their lives. And it is estimated that about 20% of adults have experienced a mood disorder at some time in their lives (Gerrig & Zimbardo, 2008).

Bipolar Disorder

Bipolar disorder (previously called manic-depressive disorder) is characterized by extreme changes in mood and behavior. There may be severe depression alternating with a distinct period in which the person has a manic episode. The mood and activity changes are very different from the child's usual behavior and different from the behavior of other children and teens. The Minnesota Association for Children's Mental Health (MACMH, 2010) describes characteristics of children and teens having a manic episode in Textbox 22.4:

TEXTBOX 22.4. SYMPTOMS RELATED TO BIPOLAR DISORDER IN CHILDREN AND ADOLESCENTS

- An expansive or irritable mood
- Depression
- Rapidly changing moods lasting a few hours to a few days
- Explosive, lengthy, and often destructive rages
- Separation anxiety
- Defiance of authority
- Hyperactivity, agitation, and distractibility
- Strong and frequent cravings, often for carbohydrates and sweets
- Excessive involvement in multiple projects and activities
- Impaired judgment, impulsivity, racing thoughts, and pressure to keep talking

- Dare-devil behaviors
- Inappropriate or precocious sexual behavior
- Delusions and hallucination
- Grandiose belief in own ability that defies the laws of logic (believing they can become a rockstar overnight, for example)

ANXIETY DISORDERS

Feeling anxious is normal, especially for adolescents when they face the various crises associated with this developmental stage. As described earlier in this book, anxiety is based on the body's natural response to threat or fear. It involves tense muscles and increased breathing and pulse rate. Here the brain is in a state of hyperarousal, with hyperawareness of sensory information or stimuli. Normal anxiety becomes a disorder when it is persistent even when the threat is not there.

Anxiety disorder is the most common mental disorder in children and adolescents, with as many as 1 out of 10 suffering from it at some time (MACMH, 2010). Girls are more likely than boys to have an anxiety disorder (Evans et al., 2005). Textbox 22.5 contains symptoms or behaviors associated with anxiety disorders in children and adolescents (MACMH, 2010).

TEXTBOX 22.5. SYMPTOMS RELATED TO ANXIETY DISORDER IN CHILDREN AND ADOLESCENTS

- Frequent school absences
- Refusal to join in social activities
- Isolating behavior
- Many physical complaints
- Excessive worry about homework or grades
- Falling grades
- Frequent bouts of tears
- Frustration
- Irritability
- Fear of new situations
- Drug or alcohol abuse
- Unrealistic obsessive fears
- Repeated unwanted thoughts and behaviors
- Tension about everyday life events

There are several different types of anxiety disorders. The following descriptions are identified by the U.S. Department of Health and Human Services as being the most common anxiety disorders affecting children and adolescents.

Generalized anxiety disorder. Students with generalized anxiety disorder (GAD) are characterized by excessive worry. This worry could be related to recent, past, or future events. Common topics of worry include past conversations or actions, schoolwork, appearance, money, their future, family health, their own health, world events, or their competence in sports or academics. Symptoms include restlessness or feeling keyed up or on edge, being easily fatigued, difficulty concentrating, irritability, muscle tension, and sleep disturbance.

Specific phobias. Students who have specific phobias suffer from an extreme and unrealistic fear or anxiety related to a specific animal, object, activity, or situation (such as flying, dogs, heights, seeing blood, dentists, clowns, etc.). Exposure to the phobic stimulus causes an immediate anxiety response, which may express itself in the form of a panic attack. This in turn causes the student to avoid fear situations. This condition can interfere with students' normal social, academic, or social activities.

Social phobias (social anxiety disorder). Students with social anxiety disorder have an excessive and persistent fear of social situations in which they feel they could be judged, ridiculed, criticized, humiliated, or embarrassed. This disorder restricts interactions with peers and can significantly interfere with students' normal academic functioning, social activities, or relationships. Also, there is distress about having the phobia itself. Social phobia can be so debilitating that it may keep some students from going to school.

Panic disorder. Students with panic disorder have repeated experiences of intense fear of impending doom or danger (panic attacks). These attacks appear without cause and are accompanied by rapid heart rate, shortness of breath, choking sensations, dizziness, nausea, sweating, a feeling of imminent death, or a feeling of depersonalization. Panic disorder is often accompanied by agoraphobia, which is a fear of public or open places. Students with panic disorder will go to great lengths to avoid a panic attack, even refusing to attend school.

Obsessive-compulsive disorder. Here the student has reoccurring, persistent, or intrusive thoughts called obsessions. These obsessions cause repetitive behaviors or mental acts that the student feels must be performed (compulsions). The compulsion could be repetitive behaviors such as hand washing, ordering, or checking. The mental acts could be things such as praying, counting, or repeating words silently. The student feels driven to perform these in response to the obsession.

Post-traumatic stress disorder. Post-traumatic stress disorder is based on having witnessed or been a part of a traumatic event or series of events such as physical or sexual abuse, violence, or a disaster (car crash, hurricanes, bombings, shooting, earth quakes, etc.). Students with PTSD present three kinds of symptoms: First, they suffer from episodes in which they reexperience the traumatic events in the form of flashbacks or reoccurring dreams. Second, they attempt to avoid any event or place associated with the original trauma. This avoidance is accompanied by feelings of numbness or reduced emotional response. Third, students with PTSD experience increased physiological arousal including difficulty falling asleep, increased irritability, or overreacting when startled.

FEEDING AND EATING DISORDERS

There are two specific types of feeding and eating disorders: anorexia nervosa and bulimia nervosa. Here students engage in abnormal eating behavior and have excessive concerns about food. These disorders primarily affect women and usually begin around the time of or soon after puberty. Also, student athletes who must make or maintain a certain weight such as wrestlers, dancers, or gymnasts may be more at risk to fall into disordered eating patterns that can then lead to full-blown eating disorders. The MACMH (2014) identifies the signs or symptoms and behaviors of an eating disorder for children and adolescents below.

- Controlled emotional expression
- Inflexible thinking
- Impaired concentration
- Withdrawn
- Concerned about eating in public
- Depressed mood or mood swings
- Self-deprecating statements
- Irritability
- Lethargy
- Fainting spells and dizziness
- Headaches
- Hiding food
- Avoiding snacks or activities that include food
- Frequent trips to the bathroom
- Refusing to eat or lying about how much was eaten
- Throwing up after meals

- Increased anxiety about weight
- Feeling cold all the time
- A need to control the environment
- Overexercising

Anorexia Nervosa

Anorexia nervosa is characterized by a refusal to maintain normal body weight. Here the student weighs less than 85% of the weight that is considered normal for that person's age, height, and body frame but stills expresses an intense fear of becoming fat. Additional symptoms include the following (NIMH 2021):

- Extremely restricted eating and/or intensive and excessive exercise
- Extreme thinness (emaciation)
- A relentless pursuit of thinness and unwillingness to maintain a normal or healthy weight
- Intense fear of gaining weight
- Distorted body image, a self-esteem that is heavily influenced by perceptions of body weight and shape, or a denial of the seriousness of low body weight

Bulimia Nervosa

Students with bulimia nervosa tend to go on eating binges followed by purging or other compensatory behaviors (APA, 2013). Additional symptoms include the following (NIMH 2021):

- Chronically inflamed and sore throat
- Swollen salivary glands in the neck and jaw area
- Worn tooth enamel and increasingly sensitive and decaying teeth (a result of exposure to stomach acid)
- Acid reflux disorder and other gastrointestinal problems
- Intestinal distress and irritation from laxative abuse
- Severe dehydration from purging
- Electrolyte imbalance (too low or too high levels of sodium, calcium, potassium and other minerals), which can lead to stroke or heart attack

SCHIZOPHRENIA

Schizophrenia is a severe and reoccurring mental disorder that usually has its onset in adolescence. It affects approximately 1% of the population and causes people to think and act strangely. Schizophrenia is recognized by delusional thinking, hallucinations, disintegration of the personality, and stymied or distorted emotional responses. Early signs may occur two to six years before onset (Evans et al., 2005). The symptoms or behaviors related to schizophrenia for children and adolescents are listed below (MACMH, 2014).

- Confused thinking
- Vivid and bizarre thoughts and ideas
- Hallucinations: hearing, seeing, feeling, or smelling things that are not real or present
- Delusions: having beliefs that are fixed and false
- Severe anxiety and fearfulness
- Extreme moodiness
- Severe problems in making and keeping friends
- Problems planning and organizing
- Feeling that people are hostile and out to get them
- Odd behavior, including behavior resembling that of a younger child
- Disorganized speech
- Lack of motivation
- Unpredictable agitation
- Poor memory

SUBSTANCE-RELATED AND ADDICTIVE DISORDERS

For people 15–24 years of age, about 50% of deaths (accidents, homicides, and suicides) involve alcohol or drug abuse (American Academy of Child and Adolescent Psychiatry, 2011). For adolescents, the main symptoms include the following (Evans et al., 2005):

- obsession-like ruminations or even craving for drugs or drug-related experiences
- compulsion-like repetitive drug-taking or drug-related behaviors to the detriment of normal behaviors
- pharmacological tolerance and observable characteristic withdrawal syndromes when there is an abrupt cessation

The DSM-5 includes disorders related to the following substances: alcohol, caffeine, cannabis, hallucinogens, inhalants, opioids, sedatives, hypnotics, and anxiolytics; stimulants (amphetamine-type substances, cocaine, and other stimulants); tobacco; and other (or unknown) substances. However, use or even abuse of any of the substances above does not necessarily indicate a disorder. It is a disorder only when use of a substance causes significant impairment or distress in social, occupational, interpersonal, or other areas of functioning. The DSM-5 symptoms for alcohol use and cannabis use disorders are listed below.

Symptoms for Alcohol Use Disorder

A problematic pattern of alcohol use leading to clinically significant impairment or distress, as manifested by at least two of the following, occurring within a 12–month period:

1. Alcohol is often taken in larger amounts or over a longer period than was intended.
2. There is a persistent desire or unsuccessful efforts to cut down or control alcohol use.
3. A great deal of time is spent in activities necessary to obtain alcohol, use alcohol, or recover from its effects.
4. Craving, or a strong desire or urge to use alcohol.
5. Recurrent alcohol use resulting in a failure to fulfill major role obligations at work, school, or home.
6. Continued alcohol use despite having persistent or recurrent social or interpersonal problems caused or exacerbated by the effects of alcohol.
7. Important social, occupational, or recreational activities are given up or reduced because of alcohol use.
8. Recurrent alcohol use in situations in which it is physically hazardous.
9. Alcohol use is continued despite knowledge of having a persistent or recurrent physical or psychological problem that is likely to have been caused or exacerbated by alcohol.
10. Tolerance, as defined by either of the following: a) a need for markedly increased amounts of alcohol to achieve intoxication or desired effect, or b) a markedly diminished effect with continued use of the same amount of alcohol.
11. Withdrawal, as manifested by either of the following: a) the characteristic withdrawal syndrome for alcohol b) alcohol (or a closely related substance, such as a benzodiazepine) is taken to relieve or avoid withdrawal symptoms.

Symptoms for Cannabis Use Disorder

A problematic pattern of cannabis use leading to clinically significant impairment or distress, as manifested by at least two of the following, occurring within a 12–month period:

1. Use of cannabis for at least a one-year period, with the presence of at least two of the following symptoms, accompanied by significant impairment of functioning and distress:
2. Difficulty containing use of cannabis—the drug is used in larger amounts and over a longer period than intended.
3. Repeated failed efforts to discontinue or reduce the amount of cannabis that is used.
4. An inordinate amount of time is occupied acquiring, using, or recovering from the effects of cannabis.
5. Cravings or desires to use cannabis. This can include intrusive thoughts and images, and dreams about cannabis, or olfactory perceptions of the smell of cannabis, due to preoccupation with cannabis.
6. Continued use of cannabis despite adverse consequences from its use, such as criminal charges, ultimatums of abandonment from spouse/partner/friends, and poor productivity.
7. Other important activities in life, such as work, school, hygiene, and responsibility to family and friends are superseded by the desire to use cannabis.
8. Cannabis is used in contexts that are potentially dangerous, such as operating a motor vehicle.
9. Use of cannabis continues despite awareness of physical or psychological problems attributed to use (e.g., anergia, amotivation, chronic cough).
10. Tolerance to xannabis, as defined by progressively larger amounts of cannabis needed to obtain the psychoactive effect experienced when use first commenced, or noticeably reduced effect of use of the same amount of cannabis
11. Withdrawal, defined as the typical withdrawal syndrome associated with cannabis, or cannabis or a similar substance is used to prevent withdrawal symptoms.

YOUTH SUICIDE

Suicide is not listed in the DSM-5 as a mental health disorder; however, it is often directly linked to mental health, most commonly depression (Gerrig & Zimbardo, 2008). Suicide is the second leading cause of death of people ages

15 to 24 (Shain, 2016). Suicide before the age of 12 or the onset of puberty is rare. Girls are twice as likely as boys to attempt suicide but boys are four times more likely to succeed (Eggen & Kauchak, 2013). Students who are lesbian, gay, bisexual, or transgender (LGBT) are significantly more likely to attempt suicide than heterosexual young people (21.5% vs. 4.2%) (Hatzenbuehler, 2011). The negative social environment that adolescents who are LGBT face may contribute to this.

Table 22.1 contains a list of risk factors associated with suicidal behavior in adolescents (Evans et al., 2005). The best predictor of suicide is previous suicide attempts, followed by depression accompanied by strong feelings of helpless and hopelessness (Craig & Baucum, 2002).

Table 22.1. Risk Factors Associated with Suicidal Behavior in Adolescents

Psychopathology	*Environment*	*Previous Suicidal Behavior*	*Sexual Orientation*
• Depression • Drug and alcohol abuse • Aggressive-impulsive behavior • Hopelessness • Pessimism • Conduct disorder (males) • Panic disorder (females)	• Firearm availability • Diminished family cohesion • Lack of parental support • Parent-child conflict • Negative life events • Child sex abuse • Suicide contagion	• Suicide attempts	• Same-sex sexual orientation

Warning Signs for Adolescent Suicide

- Withdrawal from relationships
- Withdrawal from friends or classroom and school activities
- Depression, as evidenced by persistent boredom or lack of interest in school activities
- An abrupt decline in the quality of schoolwork
- Talking about death, the hereafter, or suicide
- Giving away prized possessions, drug or alcohol abuse, personality changes such as a rise in anger, boredom, or apathy
- Comments about suicide as a solution to problems
- Unusual neglect of appearance or radical changes in personality
- Difficulty concentrating at school
- Staying away from school or other usual activities
- Complaints of physical problems when nothing is wrong

- Changes in eating or sleeping habits (Eggen & Kauchak, 2013; Papalia et al., 2004)

PROMOTING GOOD MENTAL HEALTH

The 12 recommendations below were taken from *An Educator's Guide to Children's Mental Health*, published by the Minnesota Association for Children's Mental Health (2010). These are some ideas for modeling and promoting mental fitness within a classroom. Also, they are attributes of the type of caring community that we would hope would be present in all K–12 classrooms.

1. Encourage children to talk about feelings—both their own and the feelings of others.
2. Model appropriate problem-solving and conflict resolution strategies.
3. Provide children with opportunities to practice thinking of solutions and anticipating consequences.
4. Help children identify and understand emotions they feel by giving a verbal label to emotional states.
5. Encourage children to try new things by sharing and learning together.
6. Watch for children's interests and suggest activities to support them.
7. Provide children a safe place to experiment with their growing competence and independence.
8. Provide opportunities for children to practice effective stress-reduction strategies. Even young children can learn deep breathing exercises.
9. Help children practice listening and talking.
10. Encourage children to help others.
11. Help children understand and appreciate similarities and differences among people.
12. Plan activities with the children that build a sense of belonging and community.

SUMMARY OF KEY IDEAS

- One in five students ages 9–17 have experienced a mental health issue at some time and many others remain undiagnosed or are diagnosed but left untreated.
- A mood disorder is an emotional disturbance such as severe depression (major depressive disorder) or depression alternating with mania (bipolar disorder).

- Anxiety is a natural response; however, it becomes a disorder when it is persistent and when the threat is not there and results in one or more of the following: (a) distress, pain, or suffering; (b) impairment or disability; (c) increased risk of pain, suffering, death, or less freedom for self or others; and (d) an important loss of freedom or ability to do things.
- An eating disorder is a condition where students engage in abnormal eating behavior and have excessive concerns about food to the detriment of their physical and mental health.
- The main types of eating disorders are anorexia nervosa, in which students take in insufficient nutrition and calories, and bulimia nervosa, in which students engage in binge-eating followed by some sort of purging or other compensatory behavior such as excessive exercise or fasting.
- A substance abuse disorder occurs when the use of a substance causes significant distress or impairment in social, academic, or other areas of functioning.
- Suicide is the second leading cause of death among adolescents ages 15–24.

Part V

HUMAN MOTIVATION

Chapter Twenty-Three

Motivating Factors

Motivation is an internal state that causes us to direct our attention or engage in or maintain a behavior.

MOTIVATING STUDENTS TO LEARN

All students enter kindergarten excited and eager to learn. They see themselves as able learners, whole and complete. But something happens in the next two years as they begin their journey down the 13-year educational conveyor belt. They get measured, quantified, sorted, and compared. Our educational system does something to pound all the joy of learning from these students. What happens?

Some Motivating Facts

Some facts about human motivation and learning are outlined below:

1. Learning is a natural state. All human beings learn. The human brain has evolved to create meaning out of the phenomena it encounters. We naturally try to make sense out of the world around us. It is a natural human condition. In this context, learning disabilities do not exist. In fact, much of what has been labeled a learning disability is actually a learning-certain-things disability, a learning-in-certain-ways disability, a learning-boring-and-irrelevant-things disability, a teaching-disability, or an educational systems disability.

2. Motivation and achievement are highly correlated. Note that correlation does not infer causation. That is, we cannot say that motivation causes high achievement or high achievement causes high motivation. However, we can say with confidence that there is a strong relationship between the two. Hence, motivation is something to which we should attend.

3. Motivation is highly related to positive attitude and persistence. Students who are highly motivated have a more positive attitude toward school, they cause fewer management problems, and they are more likely to persist on difficult tasks. Clearly, having students who are motivated to learn is a good thing.

4. Incentives differ. An *incentive* is any object or event that either encourages or discourages behavior. We usually think of incentives as rewards, but they could be punishments as well. Some think that motivating students to learn is just a matter of finding the right incentives. There are two things wrong with this idea:

First, simply looking for rewards and punishments to manipulate an organism into displaying the "correct" behavior is a practice that is appropriate for training mice in a Skinner box, but not so much for working with human beings in a school or classroom. Mouse trainers hand out pellets and electric shocks. Teachers do not. We should strive to be teachers, not mouse trainers.

And second, an incentive may enhance motivation in the short term, but it should not be confused with motivation. Motivation is a natural inclination to act. Incentives may enhance or diminish that natural inclination. Any human management system (school, classroom, home, or societal) that relies totally on incentives to "motivate" will eventually be found lacking. As any behaviorist will tell you, as soon as the threat of punishment or the possibility of reward disappears, the target behavior will also disappear or reappear.

5. There is often a mismatch between school goals and student goals. All students are motivated to achieve certain goals; however, students' goals are often much different from school goals. For example, many high school students are highly motivated to achieve goals related to social interactions, sports, music, relationships, self-expression, or having fun. Motivation to learn tends to be further down the list. Also, students are often motivated to achieve, but this is different from being motivated to learn (see performance vs. mastery motivation below).

6. Students will learn more and learn more deeply if they are motivated to learn. Aligning learning goals with students' goals greatly enhances learning. This means understanding our students' natural inclinations and then designing learning experiences, activities, and assignments that align with these natural inclinations. For example, middle school and high school students are negotiating social roles, peer groups, self-identity, and their own values. As such, it would be highly appropriate to design lessons and learning that uses cooperative learning activities in which the curriculum intersects with students' views, values, and interests. This does not mean that academic goals should be abandoned. It simply means that lessons, activities, and assignments should be designed around students' natural inclinations to the greatest extent possible.

7. **Choice is a powerful motivator.** When students are empowered to make choices about their learning, they are more motivated to learn. Choice includes things such as topics to study, ways to learn and demonstrate learning, books to read, things to write about, styles of writing, assignment descriptions and due dates, and ways to utilize time. Choice here does not mean total choice all the time; rather, it means some choices some of the time. As well, choice is found on a continuum (see Figure 23.1.). Instruction should always vary among the three middle choice options depending on the students and the situation.

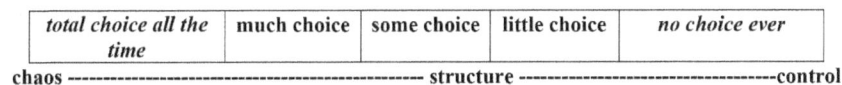

total choice all the time	*much choice*	*some choice*	*little choice*	*no choice ever*

chaos -- structure --control

Figure 23.1.   Continuum of choices.

INTRINSIC AND EXTRINSIC MOTIVATION

Intrinsic motivation is when the incentive to act comes from within the individual. This is the most powerful type of motivation for learning. *Extrinsic motivation* is when the incentive to act comes from outside the individual. This would be motivation based on rewards, prizes, or punishment (incentives). Very rarely is this an either/or proposition. High intrinsic activities can result in both high and low rewards (see Table 23.1). As well, low intrinsic activities can also result in both high and low rewards.

Table 23.1.   Extrinsic and Intrinsic Motivation

	high intrinsic	*low intrinsic*
high extrinsic	high rewards and you like doing it	high rewards but you do not like doing it
low extrinsic	low rewards but you like doing it	low rewards and you do not like doing it

There are two types of motivation to learn: *Performance motivation* is when the goal is simply to perform well, to get the letter grade, or pass the test. Here, learning is extrinsically motivated, and less learning occurs.

Mastery motivation is when the goal is to understand and master the content or skill. Here, learning is intrinsically motivated, and more learning occurs.

The lesson? We should provide interesting stuff for students to learn and teach it in ways in which they learn best. As referred to above, teaching and learning are effortless if what is taught is aligned with students' natural desire to learn. Conversely, teaching is difficult, and learning is painful when what is taught is boring or irrelevant and taught in ways that do not keep students engaged. Human beings learn more when they are intrinsically motivated to do so. As well, teachers are more effective teachers when they are intrinsically motivated—that is, when they find joy in what they do.

VALUE-EXPECTANCY THEORY

As stated previously in this book, theories do not predict behavior; rather, they help us understand behavior. The *value-expectancy theory* is one such theory that can help us understand student behavior in terms of motivation. This theory posits that students' motivation and achievement behavior is a result of their value of the activity and their expectancy of success. Put this theory in a mathematical equation and it looks like this: *value x expectancy = motivation*. And just as in any multiplication equation, if one of the factors is zero, the product will be zero.

Value

Is the activity or skill of any value to students? Do they find it of worth? Do they see themselves as using the skill in their everyday life? Is it enjoyable? Is it meaningful? Are we doing anything to devalue the skill? There are four dimensions to value: (a) attainment value, (b) intrinsic value, (c) utility value, and (d) cost belief (Schunk & Zimmerman, 2006).

Attainment value. Attainment value looks at the importance of doing well with the task. What is the value of attaining this skill? As mentioned in a previous chapter, we can enhance learning by aligning our curriculum to students' natural inclinations, curiosities, and developmental tendencies.

Intrinsic value. Intrinsic value is the amount of enjoyment derived from the task or skill.

Utility value. Utility value is the perceived usefulness of the tasks toward other goals. Do students need to use the skill? Is it useful in any way? Do they see themselves using the skill in their life outside of school? Getting students engaged in authentic experiences and activities that reflect real life will help them make real-life connections. Problem-based learning, experiential learning, discovery learning, and service learning are just some of the ways to make these connections (Johnson, 2019).

Expectancy

Does the student view himself or herself as capable of learning? Does the student expect to be able to succeed? This is very much related to self-efficacy and is described below.

SELF-EFFICACY

Self-efficacy is the belief that you can do something. It is confidence in one's ability to get things done or achieve a goal. Higher degrees of self-efficacy are correlated with higher levels of motivation, persistence, and achievement. This means that if you believe you can obtain a goal through your own efforts, you are more likely to attempt a task and persist at the task until you are successful. The opposite of self-efficacy is *learned helplessness*. Here, you have learned that no matter what you do, you will fail. This significantly hampers motivation and learning. Learned helplessness is developed through experiences with failure and frustration.

Factors That Affect Self-Efficacy

There are five factors that affect self-efficacy.

1. Past performance. Self-efficacy is derived in great part from past experiences of success and personal accomplishments. Students who have been successful in other areas or in past learning tend to see themselves as capable of learning and performing. They are more likely to try new things and more likely to persist if the task gets difficult. Students whose only school experience is failure have very low levels of self-efficacy. They are less likely to try something new and less likely to persist if the task gets difficult.

2. Verbal persuasion. Other people's assessment and encouragement can affect self-efficacy. When teachers, family, and peers express their encouragement and confidence in students' ability to succeed, they are more likely to believe they can achieve success.

3. Modeling or vicarious experiences. Self-efficacy is positively affected by seeing peers succeeding at a task. For example, if a family member or friends within the community succeeded in college, students within that community are more likely to believe that they too would succeed in college. This points to the importance of providing students with positive role models that look like them (age, background, socioeconomic status, race, ethnicity, religion, gender, sexual orientation) being successful.

4. Physiological factors. Deficiency in getting lower needs met, like hunger, fatigue, self-esteem, and safety, can negatively impact self-efficacy (see Chapter 5).

5. Social expectation. Social expectations positively impact self-efficacy. For example, we generally expect students to learn how to read, write, talk, and graduate from high school.

Implications and Applications

So what? Students with high degrees of self-efficacy are more likely to learn and attain academic and personal goals. Of the five factors above, personal accomplishment has the most impact on students' self-efficacy. Thus, an important part of an educator's job is to help students discover their unique talents and strengths and to enable them to experience success. Part of helping students experience success is teaching in ways that enable them to be successful. This means differentiating the curriculum by using multilevel teaching activities such as UDL, tier assignments, contract learning, and workshop approaches (Johnson, 2017).

ATTRIBUTION THEORY

Attribution theory explains motivation as it relates to how people determine the causal factors related to their success or failures. In other words, to what do you attribute your success or failure? Three elements are considered here: locus, stability, and controllability (see Textbox 23.1).

Locus. Internal locus of control means that you are responsible for your success. It was something you did. This enhances motivation. External locus of control looks to attribute both success and failure to something outside yourself. This inhibits motivation.

Stability. Stability is the degree to which the condition can change. An unstable attribute means that it is possible to change the outcome. This enhances motivation. A stable attribute is when you believe the outcome is stable, no matter what you do. There is nothing you can do to change the outcome. This inhibits motivation.

Controllability. Controllability is the degree to which you think you can affect change. A controllable attribute means that you believe that what you do will affect the outcome. This enhances motivation. An uncontrollable attribute means that you have no impact on the outcome. This inhibits motivation.

TEXTBOX 23.1. ATTRIBUTION FACTORS

Locus: Location or cause of performance/behavior
- A. Internal cause—within us—we can control (high motivation)
- B. External cause—outside us—we can sometimes control (low motivation)

Stability: The degree to which the cause can change
- A. Conditions or cause can change (high motivation)
- B. Conditions can't change (low motivation)

Controllability: The degree to which the individual can affect change
- A. I can control cause or conditions (high motivation)
- B. I can't control cause or conditions (low motivation)

SELF-DETERMINATION THEORY

Self-determination is a person's ability to control their environment in order to achieve their desired goals or outcome. *Self-determination theory* is a theory of human motivation that says humans are innately motivated by or driven to achieve three states of being: competence, autonomy, and relatedness (Ryan & Deci, 2000).

Competence here is the need to be successful or capable. All humans naturally want to be able to achieve and do things and be seen as competent. All humans naturally want to avoid failure or things that make them appear incompetent. As such, students need somebody, sometime to say, *"Good job!"* If students constantly experience school-related failure, they will seek out non-school things in which to be competent in order to maintain psychic stability. These could be things such as auto mechanics, computers, being a class clown, or sports. They could also be negative things such as drugs and alcohol, gangs, crime, or other destructive behaviors.

Autonomy is the need to be able to make choices about or control one's environment. Humans naturally want to do this. All students need somebody, sometime, somewhere, or somehow to say, *"It's your choice. You decide."* In the same way, humans naturally resist being controlled.

In considering motivation and classroom environment, there is a con-tinuum of structure between chaos and control similar to Figure 23.1 above. Some students need structure with more control; others need structure with less control. However, all students need structure to enable them to make positive choices. To maximize student motivation, strive always to create structure with the least amount of control necessary.

Relatedness is the ability to connect with other human beings, to have friends, or to feel loved. All students need somebody, sometime, somewhere, or somehow to say in words or actions, "*I care*," or "*I care about you.*"

You can see these three forces acting on young students every day on the playground:

> "*Watch me!*" "*Look what I can do!*" (competence)
>
> "*You're not the boss of me!*" "*Do we have to?*" (autonomy)
>
> "*Do you want to play?*" "*Can I play with you?*" (relatedness)

Chapter Twenty-Four

Perspectives On Motivation

FOUR VIEWS OR THEORIES OF MOTIVATION

This first section examines motivation from the differing theoretical perspectives. Again, a theory is a way to explain a set of facts. A theory connects data dots to explain phenomena. Different theories connect different data dots differently. Thus, each theory offers us something different to use in understanding human motivation.

Behavioral Views of Motivation

A behavioral view of human motivation describes it in terms of antecedent, behavior, and consequence (extrinsic motivation). It describes motivation in terms of what preceded the behavior (antecedent), the behavior, and then the consequence (either the reward or punishment). Rewards increase the likelihood of a behavior, and punishment decreases the likelihood of a behavior. Motivation from this perspective sees human behavior in terms of obtaining rewards and avoiding punishment.

When analyzing students' behavior (or misbehavior) it is always helpful to try to assess what rewards the behavior brings or what punishment the student might be trying to avoid. This analysis will enable you to better understand the student and the situation. However, it should be noted that behaviorism by itself provides a very shallow and incomplete view of human beings.

Cognitive Theories of Motivation

Cognitive theories of motivation focus primarily on learning. From this theoretical perspective, students are motivated to learn by the need to reduce confusion. Piaget described this process as *equilibration* (see Chapter 2). This is how it works: We start out in a state of *equilibrium* in which things make sense. When new information or novel phenomena are encountered that do not correspond to existing knowledge, a state of imbalance or *disequilibrium* is created. This is a very dissatisfying mental state. People naturally seek to create new understanding, to move from disequilibrium to equilibrium.

According to Piaget, this natural desire to make sense of the world, to create meaning out of confusion, or to move from disequilibrium back to equilibrium is the motivating force behind all learning. This process also promotes the development of new and more complex levels of knowledge. Once equilibration has been achieved, new interests and phenomena again move us to a state of disequilibrium and the cycle of learning continues.

Social or Sociocultural Learning Theories

Using the lens of social learning theory, internal self-goals are combined with external social goals to influence students' thoughts and motivate behaviors. Here, one is motivated to act in order to fit into a group, to meet social expectations, or to obtain the approval of others (parents, teachers, friends, significant others, etc.). Motivation to act could also be driven by one's need to maintain one's identity, achieve social status, or develop and maintain interpersonal relationships.

Humanistic Learning Theories of Motivation

As described in Chapter 5, Abraham Maslow described human motivation as a need to satiate or satisfy a hierarchy of needs. Based on this, he identified two levels or types of motivation: deficiency motivation and being motivation (see Textbox 24.1).

Deficiency motivation. Deficiency motivation is when a person is motivated by a perceived lack of something or a deficiency. Deficiencies related to things such as self-esteem, food, love, safety, or belonging motivate people to act to fulfill those needs. This is a low-level type of motivation.

Being motivation. Being motivation is when a person is motivated to be at their fullest state. Being motivation would be a motivation to learn or to discover (cognitive needs), to create or express (aesthetic needs), to develop one's full potential as a human being (self-actualize), or to help others or improve the human condition (transcendence).

TEXTBOX 24.1. MASLOW'S HIERARCHY OF NEEDS

B-Motivation, Being Motivation or Growth Needs

8. Transcendence = helping others
7. Self-actualization = personal growth, self-fulfillment
6. Aesthetic needs = need for beauty, balance, form, creativity; need to create and express
5. Cognitive needs = need to know, understand, learn

D-Motivation, Deficiency Motivation, Deficiency Needs—based on a lack

4. Esteem needs = achievement, status, responsibility, reputation
3. Belongingness and love needs = need to feel family affection, have relationships, or be part of the group
2. Safety needs = need for protection, security, order, law, stability, physical safety, quality of life, continuing income, protection of home
1. Biological and physiological needs = food, air, water, warmth, sleep, sex

KOHLBERG'S LEVELS OF MORAL REASONING

This section puts motivation in the context of Lawrence Kohlberg's (1984) theory of moral development. This theory describes three stages and six levels of moral reasoning (see Chapter 9).

Stage I: Pre-Conventional Levels

At the pre-conventional levels, motivation is based primarily on external circumstances (punishments and rewards).

Level 1—Punishment. At the very lowest level, you are motivated to act in order to avoid punishment.

Level 2—Rewards. At this level, you are motivated to earn a reward.

Stage II: Conventional Levels

At the conventional levels, there are some internal standards involved in motivating behavior; however, there is little reflection or personalizing of these standards.

Level 3—Social Approval. Your behavior is motivated by social conformity or the need to get approval from others.

Level 4—The Law. You are motivated by the need to conform to a law, religion, authority, or some other external mandate.

Stage III: Post-Conventional, Autonomous, or Principled Levels

This level represents the beginning of autonomous thought.

Level 5—Social Contract. At this level you are motivated to obey rules and laws only because doing so preserves social order.

Level 6—Universal Principle. Your motivation to act is based on your conscience in accordance with a set of universal principles and aligned with your highest values regardless of the consequences.

While nobody acts at any one level exclusively, Kohlberg's stages and levels helps us understand the motivation for the behaviors of students as well as the intentions behind our own behaviors.

Part VI

THE HUMAN TEACHER

Chapter Twenty-Five

Teacher as Reflective Practitioner

THE REFLECTIVE PRACTITIONER

All teachers have lessons or classes that do not go as intended; however, effective teachers reflect on their lessons to see what could have been done differently (Sadker et al., 2008). In this way, they continue to grow and develop their teaching craft (Zeichner & Liston, 1996). Reflective teaching can take place in the teaching moment, using what might be called *formative reflection*. This enables you to make changes during the teaching episode. Reflective teaching can also take place after the lesson, a form of *summative reflection*. This enables you to analyze the reasons for success or failure and to plan future teaching events.

Three dimensions of teacher reflection are described in this chapter: (a) teaching effectiveness; (b) research-based practices and theories; and (c) values, beliefs, and philosophy.

Teaching Effectiveness

The first dimension of teacher reflection is related to teacher effectiveness. Here you are concerned about the specific teaching performance and student learning (Porter et al., 2001). Questions asked might include: How did the lesson go? Did students learn? Did I achieve my purpose or learning objective? What seemed to work or go well? What could I have done differently to make the lesson better or more interesting? Was I successful in differentiating the lesson?

Research-Based Practice and Theories

The second dimension of teacher reflection is related to research and research-based theories. Here the teacher checks to see if teaching practice aligns with what is known about research-based practice and research-based theories in education. In this area there is often confusion over terms such as: *research-based practice, research-validated practice, scientifically based research,* and *evidence-based research* (Hess, 2008).

There is a common but erroneous idea related to educational research that the only type of research that counts for identifying causal relationships related to teaching is formal experimental research with dependent and independent variables and random assignment to groups. Instead, there are many different research methods and types of research that support a wide range of teaching strategies and practices. Also, there is no single research study that *proves* once and for all that a particular strategy is best. Rather, there are many thousands of research studies published in hundreds of peer-reviewed journals over many years that support a varying array of strategies, each of which might be appropriate for particular situations.

Do you have to be able to identify specific research to support everything you do in a classroom? Not if you are familiar with research-based theories. Remember that a theory is a way to explain a set of facts. Facts are created by research. Theories connect facts like dot-to-dot pictures. Different theories are formed by connecting data dots differently. You may not be able to recall or identify specific research studies; however, being familiar with research-based learning theories is a helpful first step in determining if a particular strategy or approach is supported by research.

Reflective questions here might include the following: Is this teaching practice supported by research or research-based theory? Is there a research base for the strategies or procedures used? What specific learning theory or theories might support this teaching practice? How does this teaching practice align with research-based theory?

PHILOSOPHY

A philosophy is a set of values and beliefs used to guide one's behavior. In education, you value certain types of experiences, approaches, subjects, teaching dispositions, and student outcomes. You also have a set of beliefs about how humans learn, what teaching practices are most effective, what constitutes learning, what knowledge and skills are necessary, the purpose of education in a democratic society, your purpose as a teacher and human being, and teaching ethics.

Among other things, your philosophy shapes what you teach, why you teach, how you teach, how you assess learning, and what you assess. No philosophy can be wrong if it is internalized and adopted. Your philosophy may ask big questions such as the following: What is the nature of reality? Why do we exist? What is our purpose? What is knowledge? How does one acquire knowledge? What is truth? How does knowledge affect perception? How does perception affect truth and knowledge? What is right and wrong? Questions like these are generally related to one of the big schools of educational philosophy such as essentialism, perennialism, progressivism, social reconstructionism, or existentialism.

Or, like most teachers, your educational philosophy may simply be an accumulation of your values and beliefs about teaching, learning, and education. Whether or not you are able to state it, you have a philosophy of education. Questions asked here include the following: What is it I value in a teaching and learning situation? What is it I believe to be true related to teaching and learning? What is my teaching philosophy? Am I in alignment with my teaching philosophy? Am I living my philosophy? What theories seem to best encapsulate my teaching philosophy? (The line between teaching theories and philosophies can become blurred. For example, is constructivism a philosophy or is it a learning theory?)

Note: There is no such thing as philosophical purity. Very few people are in total alignment with their philosophies all the time. A philosophy is a set of guiding principles, not a set of rules to be strictly adhered to.

Chapter Twenty-Six

Professionalism, Dispositions, and Attributes

TEACHER "PROFESSIONALISM" IN TEACHER PREPARATION

The terms *teacher professionalism* and *professional dispositions* are often used when assessing preservice and practicing teachers. But what is "teacher professionalism"? What dispositions are the "correct" ones for teachers? And who gets to decide these things?

Dispositions or Mind Control

Most teacher preparation programs address and assess three elements: knowledge, skills, and dispositions (Creasy, 2015). The dispositional element is commonly viewed as "teacher professionalism." A disposition is a state of mind that creates an inclination to think or act in certain ways. There are both positive and negative dispositions. Examples of positive dispositions include compassion, curiosity, fortitude, and honesty. Examples of negative dispositions include pessimism, laziness, dishonesty, and indifference. These dispositions are all examples of internal states of mind. Some might also consider them character traits or even values. However, some teacher preparation programs try to mandate that all preservice teachers have specific internal states of mind. Rubrics and checklists are then created to try to document and quantify these internal states of mind. But trying to control the internal state of mind of another person is a form of *mind control*. It is not healthy for the field of education to be in the business of mind control.

In most professional fields, those entering the profession must demonstrate proficient levels of knowledge and skills to be admitted. Once admitted, they must adhere to a set of professional ethics or standards for professional practice. These outline the basic norms, rules, responsibilities, and proper practices within that profession. But professionals in fields outside of education are rarely expected to display a common set of dispositions for admission to the profession. In other words, doctors, lawyers, professors, school administrators, social workers, engineers, scientists, researchers, and computer programmers are not rated on a standardized set of dispositions that reflects somebody else's vision of "professionalism." But in education, this is somehow considered appropriate. Why is this?

The Filter

"Teacher professionalism" and professional dispositions are both subjective constructs open to implicit bias in their interpretation and application. When used in teacher preparation programs they serve as a filter to ensure that certain kinds of teachers are able to pass through more easily. But who determines what dispositions are included in such a parochial filter? Who does the filter keep out? How do such filters promote or advantage some groups while disadvantaging others? Which groups might be restricted by imposing such a filter on preservice teachers?

The idea of a standardized set of attributes that all teachers should possess has its basis in cultural superiority. Here, the values of the dominant culture are seen as the "correct" ones to which all others are compared. Attributes that do not reflect those of the dominant cultural are seen as deficient or deviant. It says that one group's way of seeing and perceiving teaching is "right" and all other ways need be evaluated by how closely they match that framework. Some schools and universities will go so far as to use a rubric to quantify other people's dispositions. Preservice and practicing teachers are rated on the dispositions that have been determined to be the "right" ones. Numbers are attached to them to demonstrate their closeness to or distance from the "norm." This should all be a bit concerning.

TEACHER PROFESSIONAL ATTRIBUTES

An *attribute* is a quality or characteristic ascribed to something or someone, in this case, teachers. But can you really say that there are a standard set of attributes that all teachers should possess? Upon what data is such thinking based? Effective teachers are not standardized products. They have a variety of attributes. The attributes that one believes important for "teacher professionalism" are highly dependent on one's views, values, experiences, and teaching philosophy (see below). As well, the attributes needed for success in one teaching situation may not work well in another.

One Set of Teacher Professional Attributes

The attributes below define teacher professionalism within the context of humanistic education or humanistic learning theory (see Chapter 5). These are presented as examples. To be of use, you should not adopt them. Instead, you should identify and define your own set of teacher professional attributes based on this example.

1. You care about your students. This is the most professional of all behaviors. You want the very best for your students. You truly want them to reach their full potential as students and as humans.

2. You relate to/with your students. Teaching starts with a relationship. Until then, you are just a dancing monkey standing up in front of your students performing tricks.

3. You demonstrate unconditional positive regard (UPR) for your students, your colleagues, and yourself. To teach fully you must accept your students unconditionally. You may not always accept their behaviors, but you let them know that you accept them as human beings, just the way that they are. Your acceptance of them is not performance-based. Unconditional positive regard means that you accept people (yourself, students, other teachers, and friends) as they are—not as what you would like them to be.

4. You prepare and are prepared. If you care about your students, if you care about their learning and their impact on the world, you are prepared to teach them each day. They are worthy of your time, effort, energy, creativity, and intellect. The planning and preparation of your daily lessons, curriculum, and general classroom rules and procedures is a way of honoring your students and the teaching profession.

5. You engage in personal and professional reflection. There are three levels of reflection (see Chapter 24):

Level 1. After every teaching episode you reflect to identify those things that worked well and those things that could be done differently.

Level 2. You reflect to see if what you are doing aligns with what you know about teaching and learning. Does it reflect best practice? Can you find research or research-based theory to support what you are doing? Or is what you are doing based on "I-think-isms"?

Level 3. You reflect to see if what you are doing is in harmony with your values and your philosophy. Hence the importance of identifying said things.

6. You are willing to change and to grow. You do not see your current state as a teacher or human as an end state. You see teaching and being human both as dynamic states. To change and to grow is to be alive. To stay the same is to die. You realize that learning is never complete. You have engaged in some sort of professional development.

7. You invest in humans. An investment in yourself is the wisest sort of investment. You spend time with personal growth activities like daily reflection, personal reading, meditation, spiritual activities, or endeavors that focus on the development of interpersonal or intrapersonal intelligence, the arts, or social activities. You invest in yourself as well in terms of diet, sleep, exercise, and recreation.

What is good for the teacher is good for the student. You see your students and other humans as worth investing your time and energy in as well. Thus, in your teaching you do not simply attend to students' frontal lobes. You try to attend to the whole child: their intelligence, emotions, creativity, imagination, rationality, spirituality, intuition, and their social selves. You create activities, lessons, and experiences that might lead to their total growth as human beings.

8. You are fully present in your teaching and being. You allow your whole self to be present in your teaching. Your whole self is a tool that can help you perceive and understand your students and yourself. It also enables you to create better, more multidimensional learning experiences. You are fully present in the moment. You are focused and thinking about your teaching and your students. You allow yourself to use humor, emotions, intuition, creativity, imagination, as well as logic and knowledge in your teaching and decision-making.

When you are fully present in your teaching, teaching is fully present in your being. That is, you carry your students with you. You think about them when you are not teaching. Thus, teaching and being become intertwined.

9. You allow students to see you. You are not simply your topic or your role. You are a human being and you present this human being to your class. How much of you should be seen is always something that should be decided by you, your students, and your particular teaching situation.

10. You seek to understand. There are always reasons why humans act the way they do. No behavior can be truly understood without understanding the context in which the behavior is displayed. As stated previously, sometimes negative behavior is a healthy response to an unhealthy situation.

11. You stand up for what you believe in. When you see something detrimental to students or their learning, you are willing to stand up and speak out. Standing up for what you believe in and speaking out is not always easy. Some people may not like you. There will be some uncomfortable moments—but with the rights of a professional educator come responsibilities. You are responsible for educating the public—for speaking truth to power—for identifying effective practices. In this way, you will be an agent of change.

Attributes Left Off the List

Finally, the following list contains attributes of effective practicing teachers that will enable the field of education to continue to evolve. Many of these would enhance the quality of education in our classrooms as well as improve student learning. These would also empower teachers to become agents of change. However, you will most likely never encounter them in any school or teacher preparation program under "teacher professionalism" or "professional attributes." Why do you think that is so? Who gets to decide what goes on the list?

- innovative
- thinks outside the box
- questions traditional concepts and practices
- is not satisfied with the status quo
- holds administration accountable for decisions not in students' best interests
- speaks up in response to educational malpractice
- implements his or her values in the classroom with fidelity
- questions standards that do not adhere to a body of research-based best practice
- uses critical race theory to examine policies, procedures, curriculum, and teaching practices
- engages in serious conversations with colleagues across the field and in other fields
- pushes for social justice and racial equity
- advocates for all marginalized groups
- addresses implicit bias in a meaningful way in the school and classroom
- resists attempts to describe learning in terms of scores on standardized tests
- changes ideas with new information
- allows his or her thinking to continue to evolve
- identifies policies and practices that perpetuate systemic racism
- encourages us to live up to our educational ideals
- advocates for all students so that all can achieve their full potential
- advocates for better teacher pay and working conditions so that students can receive the very best possible education
- recognizes the importance and contributions of teachers' unions in improving the quality of education students receive
- insists that teachers be treated as professionals
- holds other teachers accountable
- engages in reflection on three levels: (a) lesson effectiveness, (b) research-basis, and (c) values and teaching philosophy
- constructively engages people with differing ideas and diverse viewpoints
- is willing to experiment and try new ideas, strategies, and techniques
- recognizes his or her professional autonomy
- seeks to align his or her teaching practice with a personal professional philosophy

APPENDICES

Appendix A

Maslow's 15 Traits of Self-Actualizing Persons

According to Maslow, mentally healthy persons are self-actualizing persons (Maslow, 1968). *Self-actualization* is the process of coming to know and understand all parts of self and realizing one's full potential on many different levels (Maslow, 1971). Maslow identified 15 traits or characteristics of self-actualizing persons:

1. Clear perception of reality. Self-actualizing persons perceive reality apart from biases, prejudices, stereotypes, or preconceived ideas and perceptions. Instead, they perceive each individual and experience objectively, to the greatest extent possible, based on the data presented. This allows for a clearer perception of reality.

2. Accepts self, others, and human nature. Self-actualizing persons have come to know all parts of self and have learned to accept both their strengths and weaknesses. While continually trying to improve, they do not spend a lot of time feeling shame, guilt, or regret about some aspect of their being or past actions. Instead, they recognize human nature, that all people have imperfections. This acceptance of themselves enables them to accept and appreciate others.

3. Spontaneous, simple, and natural. Self-actualizing persons are like children in that they behave naturally in accordance with their true nature and live in the moment. They are spontaneous, reacting to situations without pretense, without feeling the need to play a role. They're open and honest in their emotions, letting you see who they are. They don't try to play a role or be something they're not.

4. Focus on problems outside themselves. Self-actualizing persons are committed to some cause greater than themselves. They have a sense of mission that absorbs their energies.

5. Need for privacy, solitude, and independence. Self-actualizing people need privacy and solitude at times for self-reflection and to access their inner core for continued guidance and renewal.

6. Autonomous functioning. Self-actualizing people are not emotionally dependent on other people. They do not rely on other people for their happiness or need their approval. What they think is infinitely more important than what other people think of them. Thus, they are able to make their own decisions based on their values.

7. A continued freshness or appreciation of experiences. Self-actualizing people are able to appreciate certain experiences no matter how often they are repeated. For example, they can continue to appreciate a sunset, a summer day, a favorite meal, good music, or children laughing and playing. As well, self-actualizing people continue to be thankful and appreciative for what they have and what they are able to experience.

8. Mystical or "peak" experiences. Self-actualizing people are able to experience moments of profound love, happiness, truth, or harmony. These can relate to mystical or religious experiences. They also occur when one is functioning at one's highest level. Athletes and musicians, after years of experience, report instances when they are functioning at their highest when time becomes distorted, where they become completely absorbed in a task, where they perceive their experience holistically. Here they are able to focus completely, with a limited field of attention and very high concentration.

9. Social interest. Self-actualizing people have a strong interest in giving to society and helping people. They see the connectedness of all living beings and feel empathy and affection for all humans.

10. Strong interpersonal relations. Self-actualizing people are capable of stronger relationships with others than are other persons. These relationships tend to be more intense and fewer in number than those of non-actualizing persons. They are capable of greater love, deeper friendship, and more complete identification with other individuals.

11. Egalitarian values. Self-actualizing persons believe in the equality and dignity of all people regardless of social class, level of education, ability, political or religious affiliation, race or color, or sexual orientation. They do not merely tolerate differences in others; they celebrate them.

12. Strong ethical sense. Self-actualizing persons have well-defined ethical and moral standards that are used to guide them. However, their standards may not be conventional. This is because they rely on self more than social convention or custom to determine right and wrong.

13. Spontaneous and playful sense of humor. The humor of self-actualizing persons tends not to be cutting, hurtful, or hostile; rather it is spontaneous, playful, conceptual, and philosophical. This type of humor is not always recognized or appreciated by all.

14. Creativeness. Self-actualizing people are original, inventive, and innovative. They are creative, but not always in an artistic sense. They are able to play with ideas, step outside the boundaries of perceived expectations, and think in new and innovative ways in order to solve problems or create products and performances.

15. Resistance to enculturation. Self-actualizing persons are able to resist social pressures to act and think in certain ways. They are not guided by convention or tradition. Instead, they are guided by their own tastes, standards, and ideas.

Appendix B

Activities for Developing Moral Reasoning

Chapter 9 described Kohlberg's stages of moral reasoning and Gilligan's stages of ethical care. Described in this appendix are three types of activities that can be used to advance students' moral reasoning: moral dilemmas, values clarification activities, and analyzing levels and stages.

MORAL DILEMMAS

Moral dilemmas are descriptions of real-life situations in which there is a decision to be made or a problem to be solved. Students are put into small groups and asked to come to a consensus by making a decision or finding a solution. Moral dilemmas are based on the idea that children develop the capacity for moral reasoning and advance more quickly to higher levels by practicing their reasoning skills and by hearing the moral reasoning of other students (Vygotsky's sociocultural theory). Thus, the decisions or solutions children come up with are not as important as the reasoning that goes along with it. Teachers may ask questions related to how students came to certain decisions, but they should not correct, evaluate, or validate students' responses and they should not lead students toward a predetermined choice or response. This would defeat the whole purpose of the moral dilemma.

What if violent, racist, sexist, or other inappropriate ideas are put forth by students? If these types of solutions appear, it becomes a teaching moment to help students understand why the ideas might be inappropriate. While hateful and harmful ideas should not be tolerated in any situation under any circumstance, simply quashing them without explanation is not as productive as making it a teaching situation.

Moral dilemmas should be, to the greatest extent possible, developmentally appropriate and based on the lives and experiences of your students. You can design your own based on issues the arise within the classroom, school, or community. There are two other sources. The first is look for appropriate dilemmas in advice columns. The second is to do a Google search using terms such as moral dilemma, or moral dilemma students, or ethical dilemma students. One cautionary note here: You can find online moral dilemmas that are moralistic, propagandizing, or that try to push students toward an obvious answer. These are to be avoided. Moral dilemmas should not be moralistic. A good moral dilemma does not have an obvious answer. That is why it is a dilemma. Textbox B.1 is an example of a moral dilemma found online.

TEXTBOX B.1. EXAMPLE OF A MORAL DILEMMA

EXAMPLE: The Streetcar

A streetcar is driving downhill on a track. The streetcar can't stop because the brakes were damaged by a crazy man. Down the track, six homeless people are waiting in a fear. They were tied to the track by the same crazy guy.

Here's the good news. You can save the six people from death by turning a switch, which will send the streetcar down a different track. Unfortunately, there is one person, who happens to be a world-famous doctor, tied to that track.

What do you do: turn the switch or do nothing?

Source: https://www.eslwriting.org/moral-dilemma-critical-thinking-english-lesson/

Moral dilemmas do not always have to address issues of great ethical concern. They can address issues with which students struggle in their own very real lives. The moral dilemma in Textbox B.2 is one such example. In using moral dilemmas that deal with gender, it is sometimes good to have some mixed-gender groups and some single-gender groups. At the end of the activities, each group should report their decision and thinking to the larger group.

TEXTBOX B.2. EXAMPLE OF A REAL-LIFE MORAL DILEMMA

EXAMPLE

There is a boy I like and I think he likes me too but he will never make a move and just seems nervous. What should I do?

Moral dilemmas are also good for writing prompts as students can describe and support their ideas when they write. When using moral dilemmas for writing, always start with a small-group discussion. Instead of reporting to the larger group, students write to describe and support their decision.

VALUES CLARIFICATION ACTIVITIES

Values clarification is a strategy designed to help students identify, examine, and clarify their own values (Johnson, 2006). In the past, these activities have been mischaracterized as trying to tell students that there is no such thing as right or wrong (see the definition of morality in Chapter 9). This is not the case. Instead, these types of activities provide a platform for students to define and develop their own set of values and identify behaviors that support their values. This is always more powerful and long-lasting than simply telling them what they should value or how they should behave.

Values clarification activities usually involve defining, listing, ranking, or rating things that students' value. These activities come in many different forms, but they should have some or all of the following four characteristics:

- Students' insights and ideas are respected. Teachers do not correct, evaluate, or validate students' responses.
- Students are free to make choices. Teachers do not lead students toward a predetermined choice or response.
- There is a discussion or sharing of ideas either before or after the activity.
- Students are encouraged to consider both the positive and negative consequences of their choices.

Below are ideas for possible values clarification activities. Keep in mind the developmental level of your students in adapting each activity to your teaching situation.

Define that which is valued. Students list or define five to ten things that they value. You could do this in a number of different categories such as material things, virtues, personal characteristics, experiences, activities, or people. A common starting activity is to have them list five physical objects they value. After sharing their lists, in small groups or in a journal, ask students what their valued objects might say about them or who they are.

In subsequent lessons, have students list or define what they value related to friendship traits, jobs or occupations, social skills, student responsibilities, student rights, human rights, topics of interests, leisure activities, entertainment options, books, TV shows, or movies. These should always be followed by some sort of processing activity in which students are asked, "What does this tell you about who you are and what you value?" Any of these activities can be extended by asking students to rank the items in their lists from most important to least important and having them justify or support their top choices.

Ranking personal values or virtues. Given a list of personal values or virtues such as honesty, compassion, and hard work, ask students to rank them from most important to least. They should then describe their reasons for picking their top two values. This works well as a small-group activity because it always invites good conversations. The answers students come up with are not nearly as important as the preceding conversation. It is in conversation that students must clarify and communicate that which they value as well as listen to and learn from others.

Ranking experiences. In a large group, generate a list of present or future experiences that students find enjoyable such as playing football, getting a driver's license, eating dinner with the family, or talking with friends. Individually or in a small group, ask students to rank them from most important to them to least important. They should then describe their reasons for picking their top two experiences. This kind of activity helps you to understand your students and see what is of value to them. Make sure you do not diminish students' choices here.

Ranking decisions. Present your students with a description of a problem or a decision that must be made in a particular situation. This problem or decision can be taken from current events, history, or science, or from a trade book, story, television show, or movie. Then give students three to eight solutions or decisions relative to this problem. Ask them to rate or rank the decisions and to describe the value reflected in their top choice. This lesson can be extended on subsequent days by having students generate a list of their own solutions or decisions. They can also rank their solutions from most compassionate to least, most effective to least, most economic to least, most enjoyable to least, etc.

ANALYZING LEVELS AND STAGES

The last type of activity to develop students' moral reasoning invites them to examine behaviors, analyze contexts, and then assess the level of moral reasoning used to motivate that behavior. Students could analyze behaviors from history, current events, trade books or narrative texts, or movies and popular TV shows.

You can help to develop students' critical thinking here by first modeling the type of thinking necessary for this. Here, cognitive modeling would be used to analyze a behavior. The analysis here is not based on conjecture, but on clues or information. The steps should be taught explicitly and modeled. They are as follows: First define the behavior, then identify and list clues or supporting information. Finally, determine the level of moral reasoning used. A simple graphic organizer like that in Textbox B.3 can be used here.

TEXTBOX B.3. GRAPHIC ORGANIZER FOR CRITICAL THINKING RELATED TO LEVELS AND STAGES

Behavior:
Clues/Information:
Stage:

key: 1 = punishment; 2 = rewards; 3 = social approval; 4 = the law; 5 = social contract; 6 = universal principle

References

Abiodun, S. (2019). "Seeing color": A discussion of the implications and applications of race in the field of neuroscience. *Frontiers in Human Neuroscience, 13,* 1–4.

Allington, R. (1994). What's so special about special programs for children who find learning to read difficult? *Journal of Reading Behavior, 26,* 95–115.

Allington, R. L. (2011). Research on reading/learning disability interventions. In S. J. Samuels and A. E. Farstrup's (Eds.). *What research has to say about reading instruction* (4th ed.). International Reading Association.

Allington, R. (2013). What really matters when working with struggling readers. *The Reading Teachers, 66,* 520–530. https://doi.org/10.1002/TRTR.1154

Allington, R., & McGill-Franzen, A. (2017). Comprehension difficulties and struggling readers. In S. Israel (Ed.). *Handbook of research on reading comprehension* (2nd ed., pp. 271–292). The Guilford Press.

American Academy of Child and Adolescent Psychiatry. (2011). *Alcohol and drug use.* http://www.aacap.org/

American Psychiatric Association. (2013). *Diagnostic and statistical manual of mental disorders* (5th ed).

Annamma, S. A., Connor, D., & Feri, B. (2013). Dis/ability critical race studies (DisCrit): Theorizing at the intersections of race and dis/ability. *Race, Ethnicity and Education, 16,* 1–3. DOI: 10.1080/13613324.2012.73511

Annamma, S. A., Connor, D., & Ferri B. (2016). Dis/ability critical race studies (DisCrit): Theorizing at the intersections of race and dis/ability. In E. Taylor, D. Gillborn, & G. Ladson-Billings (Eds). *Foundations of critical race theory in education* (2nd ed., pp. 198–219). Routledge.

Artiles, A. (2017). Untangling the racialization of disabilities: An intersectional critique across disability models. *Du Bois Review, 10,* 329–347.

Ansley, F. (1997). White supremacy (and what we should do about it). In R. Delgado & J. Stefanic (Eds). *Critical white studies: Looking behind the mirror* (pp. 592–595). Temple University Press.

Auger, R. (2011). *The school counselor's mental health sourcebook: Strategies to help students succeed.* Corwin.

Baldwin, J. (1991). *The fire next time.* Random House.

Banks, J. A. (2002). *An introduction to multicultural education.* Allyn & Bacon.

Banks, J. (2017). "These people are never going to stop labeling me": Educational experience of African American male students labeled with learning disabilities. *Equity and Excellence in Education, 50,* 96–97.

Bauman, J. F. (2009). Vocabulary and reading comprehension: The nexus of meaning. In S. E. Israel & G. G. Duffy (Eds.). *Handbook of research on reading comprehension* (pp. 323–346). Routledge.

Bell, D. A. (1992) *Faces at the bottom of the well: The permanence of racism.* Basic Books.

Benner, S., Bell, S., & Broemmel, A. (2011). Teacher education and reading disabilities. In A. McGill-Franzen & R. Allington (Eds.). *Handbook of reading disability research* (pp. 68–79). Routledge.

Bentum, K., & Aaron, P. (2003) Does reading instruction in learning disability resource rooms really work?: A longitudinal study. *Reading Psychology, 24,* 361–382. DOI: 10.1080/02702710390227387

Bergelson, E., & Swingley, D. (2012). At 6–9 months, human infants know the meaning of many common nouns. *Proceedings of the National Academy of Sciences, 109*(9), 3253–3258. DOI: 10.1073/pnas.1113380109

Blanchett, W. (2006). Disproportionate representation of African American students in special education: Acknowledging the role of white privilege and racism. *Educational Research, 35,* 24–28.

Blachowicz, C. L. Z., & Fisher, P. (2006). *Teach vocabulary in all classrooms,* (3rd ed.). Upper Pearson Education, Inc.

Borich, G. D. (2007). *Effective teaching methods* (6th ed.). Pearson.

Bowe, F. (2005). *Making inclusion work.* Pearson.

Bruner, J. (1966). *Toward the theory of instruction.* Harvard University Press.

Bruner, J. (1977). *The process of education.* Harvard University Press.

Brownell, M., Klingner, J., Leko, M., & Galman, S (2010). Differences in beginning special education teachers: The influence of personal attributes, preparation, and school environment on classroom reading practices. *Learning Disability Quarterly, 33,* 75–92.

Brownell, M., Ross, D., Colón, E., & McCallum, C. (2005). Critical features of special education teacher preparation: A comparison with general teacher education. *The Journal of Special Education, 38,* 242–252.

Brooks-Immel, D. R., & Murray, S. B. (2017). Color-blind contradictions and black/white binaries: White academics upholding whiteness. *Humbolt Journal of Social Relations, 39,* 315–333.

Brown, K., & Jackson, D. D. (2013). The history and conceptual elements of critical race theory. In M. Lyn and A. Dixson (Eds.). *Handbook of critical race theory in education* (pp. x–x). Routledge.

Center for American Progress (2021). *The basic facts about children in poverty.* https://www.americanprogress.org/issues/poverty/reports/2021/01/12/494506/basic-facts-children-poverty/

Checkley, K. (1997). The first seven . . . and the eighth: A conversation with Howard Gardner. *Educational Leadership, 55*, 8–13.

Chomsky, N. (1968). *Language and mind.* Orlando, FL: Harcourt, Brace & World.

Chi, M. T., Feltovish, P. J., & Glaser, R. (1981). Categorization and representation of physics problems by experts and novices. *Cognitive Science, 5*, 121–152.

Conner, D. (2017). Who is responsible for racialized practices evident within (special) education and what can be done to change them? *Theory into Practice, 56*, 226–233.

Connor, D., Cavendish, W., Gonzalez, T., & Jean-Pierce, P. (2019). Is a bridge even possible over troubled waters? The field of special education negates the overrepresentation of minority students: A DisCrit analysis. *Race, Ethnicity and Education, 22*, 723–745.

Corpley, A. (2000). Defining and measuring creativity: Are creativity tests worth using? *Roeper Review, 23*, 72–79.

Council for Accreditation of Educator Preparation. (2018). *CAEP 2018 K-6 elementary teacher preparation standards.* http://caepnet.org/accreditation/caep-accreditation/caep-k-6-elementary-teacher-standards

Council for the Accreditation of Educator Preparation. (2019). *CAEP 2018 K-6 elementary teacher preparation standards: Initial licensure programs.* CAEP. http://caepnet.org/~/media/Files/caep/standards/2018–caep-k-6–elementary-teacher-prepara.pdf?la=en

Council for Exceptional Children. (2020). *Initial special education preparation standards.* https://exceptionalchildren.org/standards/initial-special-education-preparation-standards

Coutinho, M. J., Oswal, D. P., & Best, A. M. (2002). The influence of sociodemographics on the disproportionate identification of minority students as having learning disabilities. *Remedial and Special Education, 23*, 49–59.

Cunningham, W., Johnson, M., Ray, C., Gatenby, J., Gore, J., & Banaji, M. (2004). Separable neural components in the processing of black and white faces. *Psychological Science, 15*, 306–313.

Creasy, K. (2015). Defining professionalism in teacher education programs. *Journal of Education & Social Policy, 2*, 23–25.

Cruz, R., Manchanda, S., Firestone, A., & Rodl, J. (2020). An examination of teachers' culturally responsive teaching self-efficacy. *Teacher Education and Special Education, 43*, 197–214.

Csikszentmihalyi, M. (1990). *Flow: The psychology of optimal experience.* Harper-Prennial.

Csikszentmihalyi, M. (1994). The domain of creativity. In D. Feldman, M. Csikszentmihalyi, & H. Gardner (Eds.). *Changing the world: A framework for the study of creativity* (pp. x–x). Praeger Publishing.

Davis, G. A., & Rimm, S. B. (1998) *Education of the gifted and talented* (4th ed.). Allyn and Bacon.

DeCarvalho, R. (1991). The humanistic paradigm in education. *The Humanistic Psychologist, 19*(1), 88–104.

DeGroot, A. D. (1965). *Thought and choice in chess.* Mouton.

Delgado, R., & Stefancic, J. (2017). *Critical race theory: An introduction* (3rd ed). New York University Press.

Denton, C. A., Vaugh, S., & Fletcher, J. M. (2003). Bringing research-based practice in reading intervention to scale. *Learning Disabilities Research and Practice, 18*(3), 201–211.

Diaz-Lefebvre, R. (2006). Learning for understanding: A faculty-driven paradigm shift in learning, imaginative teaching, and creative assessment. *Community College Journal of Research & Practice, v30*, 135–137.

Duncker, K. (1945). On problem solving. *Psychological Monographs, 58*, i–113. DOI: 10.1037/h0093599

Dunbar-Ortiz, R. 2014). *An indigenous people's history of the United States*. Beacon Press.

Eberhardt, J. (2005). Imaging race. *American Psychologist, 60*, 181–190.

Eggen, P., & Kauchak, D. (2020). *Using educational psychology in teaching* (11th ed.). Pearson.

Eggen, P., & Kauchak, D. (2013). *Educational psychology: Windows on classrooms* (9th ed.). Pearson.

Eppley, K., & Dudley-Marling, C. (2018). Does direction instruction work?: A critical assessment of direct instruction research and its theoretical perspective. *Journal of Curriculum and Pedagogy, 14*, 1–20. DOI: 10.1080/15505`70.2018.143821

Evens, D. L., Foa, E. B., Gur, R. E., Hendin, H., O'Brien, C. P., Seligman, M., & Walsh, B. T. (2005). *Treating and preventing adolescent mental health disorders*. Oxford University Press.

Feldhusen, J. F. (1995). Creativity: Knowledge base, metacognitive skills, and personality factors. *Journal of Creative Behavior, 29*, 255–268.

Feldman, D. H., Csikzentmihalyi, M., & Gardner, H. (1994). *Changing the world: A framework for the study of creativity*. Praeger Publishing.

Fish, R. E. (2019). Standing out and sorting in: Exploring the role of racial composition in racial disparities in special education. *American Education Research Journal, 56*, 2578–2608.

Freeman, S., & Alkin, M. (2000). Academic and social attainments of children with mental retardation in general education and special education settings. *Remedial and Special Education, 21*(1), 3–18.

Freire, P. (1993) *Pedagogy of the oppressed*. Penguin Books.

Fries, P. H. (2008). Words, context, and meaning in reading. In A. Flurky, E. Paulson, & K. Goodman (Eds.). *Scientific realism in studies of reading* (pp. 53–82). Lawrence Erlbaum Associates.

Fulbright-Anderson, K., Lawrence, K., Sutton, S., Susi, G., & Kubi, A. (2005). *Structural racism and youth development: Issues, challenges, and implications*. Aspen Institute Roundtable on Community Change and Advisors to the Project on Structural Racism and Community Revitalization.

Gallagher, J. J., & Gallagher, S. A. (1994). *Teaching the gifted child* (4th ed.). Allyn and Bacon.

Gardner, H. (1993). *Multiple intelligences: The theory in practice*. Basic Books.

Gardner, H. (1994). *Creating minds*. Basic Books.

Gardner, H. (1999) *Intelligence reframed: Multiple intelligences for the 21st century.* Basic Books.

Gay, G. (2018). *Culturally responsive teaching: Theory, research, and practice.* Teachers College Press.

Gazzaniga, M. S., Ivry, R. B., & Mangun, G. R. (2002). *Cognitive neuroscience: The biology of the mind* (2nd ed). W. W. Norton & Company.

Gerrig, R., & Zimbardo, P. (2008). *Psychology and life* (18th ed). Pearson.

Gillborn, D. (2013). The policy of inequity: Using CRT to unmask white supremacy in education policy. In M. Lyn and A. Dixson (Eds.). *Handbook of critical race theory in education* (pp. 129–139). Routledge.

Goleman, D. (1994). *Emotional intelligence.* Bantam Books.

Good, T., & Brophy, J. (1995). *Contemporary educational psychology* (5th ed.). Longman.

Graves, M. F., & Silverman, R. (2011). Interventions to enhance vocabulary development. In A. McGill-Franzen & R. L. Allington's (Eds.). *Handbook of reading disability research* (pp. x–x). Routledge.

Hall, C., & Johnson, A. (1994) Module A5: Planning a test or examination. In B. Imrie & C. Hall (Eds.). *Assessment of student performance* (pp. x–x). University Teaching Development Centre, Victoria University of Wellington.

Hammond, Z. (2015). *Culturally responsive teaching & the brain: Promoting authentic engagement and rigor among culturally and linguistically diverse students.* Corwin.

Hamre, B. K., & Pianta, R. C. (2005). Can instructional emotional support in the first grade classroom make a difference for children at rish of school failure? *Child Development, 76,* 949–967.

Harry, B., & Klinger, J. (2014). *Why are so many minority students in special education? Understanding race and disability in schools* (2nd ed.) Teachers College Press.

Harp, B., & Brewer, J. A. (2005). *The informed reading teacher: Research-based practice.* Pearson Prentice Hall.

Harung, H. S., Heaton, D. P., Graff, W. W., & Alexander, C. N. (1996). Peak performance and higher states of consciousness: A study of world-class performers. *Journal of Managerial Psychology, 11,* 3–23.

Hatzenbuehler, M. (2011). The social environment and suicide attempts in lesbian, gay, and bisexual youth. *Pediatrics, 127.* The American Academy of Pediatrics. https://media.scpr.org/documents/2011/04/19/The_Social_Environment_and_Sui cide_Attempts_in_Lesbian_Gay_and_Bisexual_Youth_1.pdf

Haycock, K., & Crawford, C. (2008). Closing the teacher quality gap. *Educational Leadership, 65,* 14–19.

Hawkins, J. (2004). *On intelligence.* Times Books.

Hess, F. M. (2008). The politics of knowledge. *Phi Delta Kappan, 89*(5), 354–356.

Hinton, C., Miyamota, K., & Dell-Chiese, B. (2008). Brain research, learning and emotions: Implications for education research, policy and practice. *European Journal of Education, 43,* 87–102.

Irizarry, J. (2010). For us, by us: A vision for culturally sustaining pedagogies forwarded by Latinx youth. In D. Paris & H. Alim (Eds.). *Culturally sustaining pedagogies: Teaching and learning for justice in a changing world* (pp. 83–98). Teachers College Press.

Jennings, J. H., Caldwell, J. S., & Lerner, J. W. (2010). *Reading problems: Assessment and teaching strategies* (6th ed.). Allyn & Bacon.

Jensen, E. (2009). *Teaching with poverty in mind: What being poor does to kids' brains and what schools can do about it.* ASCD.

Jensen, E. (2013). How poverty effects classroom engagement. *Educational Leadership, 70,* 24–30.

Johnson, A. (2000). *Up and out: Using creative and critical thinking skills to enhance learning.* Allyn and Bacon.

Johnson, A. (2008). *Teaching reading and writing: Research-based strategies for teachers, tutors, parents, and paraprofessionals.* Rowman & Littlefield.

Johnson, A. (2009). *Making connections in elementary and middle school social studies* (2nd ed). SAGE Publications.

Johnson, A. (2013). *Educational psychology: Theories of learning and human development.* National Social Science Press.

Johnson, A. (2016). *10 essential instructional elements for students with reading difficulties: A brain-friendly approach.* Corwin.

Johnson, A. (2017). *Teaching strategies for all teachers.* Rowman & Littlefield.

Johnson, A. (2019). *Essential learning theories and their applications.* Rowman & Littlefield.

Johnson, A. (2021). *Designing meaning-based interventions for reading.* Guilford Press.

Johnson, A. (2022). In search for an understanding of culturally responsive teaching. In T. Flowers (Ed.). *The urban education sourcebook* (pp. x–x). Cambridge Scholars Publishing.

Kendi, I. (2019). *How to be an antiracist.* One World Press.

Klingner, J., Urbach, J., Golos, D., Brownell, M., & Menon, S. (2010). Teaching reading in the 21st century: A glimpse at how special education teachers promote reading comprehension. *Learning Disability Quarterly, 33,* 59–74.

Kornhaber, M. (2004). Multiple intelligences: From the ivory tower to the dusty classroom—but why? *Teachers College Record, 106,* 67–76.

Kohli, R., Pizarro, M., & Nevarez, A. (2019). The "new racism" of K-12 schools: Centering critical research on racism. *Review of Research in Education, 41,* 182–202.

Ladson-Billings, G. (2014). Culturally relevant pedagogy 2.0: A.k.a. the remix. *Harvard Educational Review, 85,* 74–84.

Ladson-Billings, G. (2016). Critical race theory—What it is not! In E. Taylor, D. Gillborn, & G. Ladson-Billings (Eds). *Foundations of critical race theory in education* (2nd ed., pp. 345–356). Routledge.

Ladson-Billings, G. (2016). Just what is critical race theory and what's it doing in a nice field like education? In E. Taylor, D. Gillborn, & G. Ladson-Billings (Eds). *Foundations of critical race theory in education* (2nd ed., pp. 15–30). Routledge.

Ladson-Billings, G. (2017). The (r)evolution will not be standardized: Teacher education, hip hop pedagogy, and culturally relevant pedagogy 2.0. In D. Paris & H. Alim (Eds.). *Culturally sustaining pedagogies: Teaching and learning for justice in a changing world* (pp. 141–156). Teachers College Press.

Lane. H. B., & Allen, S. A. (2010). The vocabulary-rich classroom: Modeling sophisticated word use to promote word consciousness and vocabulary growth. *The Reading Teacher, 63*, 362–370.

LeDoux, J. (2002). *Synaptic self: How our brains became who we are.* Penguin Books.

LeDoux, J. (2015). *The emotional brain: the mysterious underpinnings of emotional life.* Simon & Schuster.

Lee, S., & Walsh, D. (2017). Socially just and sustaining pedagogy for diverse immigrant youth: Possibilities, challenges, and directions. In D. Pars & H. Alim (Eds). *Culturally sustaining pedagogies: Teaching and learning for justice in a changing world* (pp 191–206). Teachers College Press.

Linley, J. (2018). Racism here, racism there, racism everywhere: The racial realities of minoritize peer socialization agents at a historically white institution. *Journal of College Student Development, 59*, 21–36.

Lipshitz, A., & Waingortin, M. (1995). Getting out of ruts: A laboratory study of a cognitive model of reframing. *Journal of Creative Behavior, 29*, 151–172.

Lynch, M. D., & Harris, C. D. (2001). *Fostering creativity in children, K-8.* Allyn and Bacon.

Machazo, G. M., & Motz, L. L. (2005). Brain research: Implications to diverse learners. *Science Educator, 14*, 56–60.

Marzano, R. J., Brandt, R. S., Hughes, C. S., Jones, B. F., Presseisen, B. R., Rankin, S. C., & Suhor, C. (1988). *Dimensions of thinking.* The Association for Supervision and Curriculum Development.

Maslow, A. (1968). *Toward a psychology of being.* John Wiley & Sons.

Maslow, A. (1971). *The farther reaches of human nature.* Viking Press.

May, R. (1975). *The courage to create.* Norton.

Mayer, R. E., & Wittrock, M. C. (2006). Problem solving. In P. A. Alexander & P. H. Winne (Eds.). *Handbook of educational psychology* (pp. x–x). Erlbaum.

Miller, J. (2001). *The holistic curriculum* (2nd ed). Buffalo, NY: University of Toronto Press.

Minnesota Association for Children's Mental Health. (2010). *An educator's guide to children's mental health.*

Minnesota Association for Children's Mental Health. (2014). *Fact Sheets.*

Minnesota Department of Education. (2021, March, 29). *Gifted education.* https://education.mn.gov/mde/fam/gifted/

Moody, S., Vaugh, S., & Hughes, M. (2000). Reading instruction in the resource room: Set up for failure. *Exceptional Children, 66*(3), 305–316.

NAEYC. (2020). Developmentally appropriate practice. National Association for the Education of Young Children. https://www.naeyc.org/resources/topics/dap

National Center for Education Statistics. (2019*). National Assessment of Educational Progress: An overview of NAEP*. Institute of Education Sciences, U.S. Department of Education. https://www.nationsreportcard.gov/

National Center for Education Statistics. (2019). *Status and trends in the education of racial and ethnic groups 2018*. U.S. Department of Education.

National Institute of Mental Health. (2021). *Child and adolescent mental health*. URL

Oliver M. (1996). *Understanding disability: From theory to practice*. St. Martin's Press.

Olson, M. H., & Hergenhan, B. R. (2009). *An introduction to theories of learning* (8th ed.). Pearson.

Ormrod, J. (2012). *Human learning* (6th ed.). Pearson.

Ormrod, J. E., Anderman, E. M., & Anderman, L. (2020). *Educational psychology: Developing learners* (10th ed). Pearson.

Ortiz, P. (2018). *An African American and Latinx history of the United States*. Beacon Press.

Patterson, C. H. (1987). What has happened to humanistic education? *Michigan Journal of Counseling and Development, 18*, 9–10.

Patterson, K. (19770. *A bridge to Terabithia*. HarperCollins.

Park, J., Turnbull, A. P., & Turnbull, H. R. (2002). Impacts of poverty on quality of life in families of children with disabilities. *Exceptional Children, 68*(2), 151–170.

Paulson, G. (2009). *Hatchet*. Simon & Schuster Books.

Peterson, M., & Hittie, M. (2010). *Inclusive teaching: The journey towards effective schools for all learners.* Merrill.

Perfetti, C. A., & Stafura, J. (2014). Word knowledge in a theory of reading comprehension. *Scientific Studies of Reading, 18*, 22–37. https://doi-org.ezproxy.mnsu.ed u/10.1080/10888438.2013.827687

Pfeiffer, S. (2000). Emotional intelligence: Popular but elusive construct. *Roeper Review, 23*, 138–142.

Piirto, J. (1994). *Talented children and adults: Their development and education*. Macmillan.

Porter, A. C., Youngs, P., & Odden, A. (2001). Advances in teacher assessment and their uses. In V. Richardson (Ed.). *Handbook of research on teaching* (p. 259–297). American Educational Research Association.

Purves, D., Brannon, E. M., Cabeza, R., Huettel, S. A., LaBar, K. S., Platt, M. L., & Woldorff, M. G. (2008). *Principles of cognitive neuroscience*. Sinauer Associates.

Rogers, C. R. (1961). *On becoming a person: A psychotherapist's view of psychotherapy*. Houghton Mifflin.

Rogers, C. R., & Freiberg, H. J. (1994). *Freedom to learn* (3rd ed.). Merrill/Macmillan.

Ronquillo, J., Denson, T., Lickel, B., Lu, Z., Nomdy, A., & Maddox, K. (2007). The effects of skin tone on race-related amygdala activity: An fMRI investigation. *SCAN, 2*, 39–44.

Rumberge, R. (2013). *Poverty and high school dropouts: The impact of family and community poverty on high school dropouts*. American Psychological Association. https://www.apa.org/pi/ses/resources/indicator/2013/05/poverty-dropouts

Ryan, R. M., & Deci, E. (2000). Self-determination theory and the facilitation of intrinsic motivation, social development, and well-being. *American Psychologist, 55*, 68–78. DOI: 10.1037//0003–066x.55.1.68

Sadker, D., Sadker, M., & Zettleman, K. R. (2008). *Teachers, schools, and society* (8th ed.). McGraw-Hill.

Salend, S. (2004). *Creating inclusive classrooms* (5th ed.). Pearson.

Sankar, A., Costafreda, S., Marangell, L., & Fu, C. (2018). Other races' effects on amygdala response during affective facial processing in major depression. *Neuroscience letters, 662*, 381–384.

Sayeski, K., Budin, S., & Bennett, K. (2015). Promising practices in the preparation of special educators to provide reading instruction. *Intervention in School and Clinic, 51*, 82–89.

Schunk, D. H., & Zimmerman, B. J. (2006). Competence and control beliefs: Distinguishing the means and ends. In P. A. Alexander & P. H. Winne (Eds.). *Handbook of educational psychology* (pp. 349–367). Erlbaum.

Shain, B. (2016). Suicide and suicide attempts in adolescents. *Pediatrics, 138*, 669–676. DOI: https://doi.org/10.1542/peds.2016–1420

Shifrer, D., Muller, C., & Callahan, R. (2016). Disproportionality and learning disabilities: Parsing apart race, socioeconomic statues, and language. *Journal of Learning Disabilities, 44*, 246–257.

Sisk, D., & Torrance, E. P. (2001). *Spiritual intelligence: Developing higher consciousness*. Creative Education Foundation Press.

Sousa, D. A. (2011). *How the brain learns* (4th ed). Corwin Press.

Starko, A. J. (2005). *Creativity in the classroom: Schools of curious delight* (3rd. ed). Lawrence Erlbaum.

Stahl. S. (1999). *Vocabulary development*. Brookline Books.

Stanley, D., Phelps, E., & Banaji, M. (2008). The neural basis of implicit attitudes. *Current Directions in Psychological Science, 17*, 164–170.

Strauss, S. L., Goodman, K. S., & Paulson, E. J. (2009). Brain research and reading: How emerging concepts in neuroscience support a meaning construction view of the reading process. *Education Research and Review, 5*(2), pp. 21–33.

Sternberg, R. J. (1985). *Beyond IQ: A triarchic theory of intelligence*. Cambridge University Press.

Sternberg, R. (1996). *Successful intelligence: How practical and creative intelligence determine success in life*. Plume.

Sternberg, R. J. (2003). A broad view of intelligence: A theory of successful intelligence. *Consulting Psychology Journal: Practice and Research, 55*, 139–154.

Sternberg, R. J., & Grigorenka, E. (2000). *Teaching for successful intelligence*. Skylight Professional Development.

Sternberg, R. J., & Lubart, T. (1991). Creative giftedness: A multivariate investment approach. *Gifted Child Quarterly, 37*, 7–15.

Sternberg, R. J., & Williams, W. M. (2002). *Educational psychology*. Pearson Education.

Swartz, R. J., & Perkins, D. N. (1990). *Teaching thinking: Issues and approaches*. Midwest Publications.

Swanson, E. (2008). Observing reading instruction for students with learning disabilities: A synthesis. *Learning Disabilities, 31*, 115–133.

Swanson, E., & Vaughn, S. (2010). An observation study of reading instruction provided to elementary students with learning disabilities in the resource room. *Psychology in the Schools, 47*, 481–492. DOI: 10.1002/pits.20484

Sylwester, R. (2000). Unconscious emotions. *The Science of Learning, 58*, 20–24.

Taylor, E. (2016). The foundations of critical race theory in education: An introduction. In E. Taylor, D. Gillborn, & G. Ladson-Billings (Eds). *Foundations of critical race theory in education* (2nd ed., pp 1–11). Routledge.

Torrance, E. P. (1992). The beyonders in a thirty year longitudinal study of creative achievement. *Roeper Review, 15*, 131–139.

Torrance, E. P. (1993). Understanding creativity: Where to start? *Psychological Inquiry, 4*, 232–234.

Torrance, E. P. (1999). *Torrance Test of Creative Thinking: Norms and technical manual.* Scholastic Testing Services.

Tuckett, D. (2019) Ideas prevented from becoming conscious: On Freud's unconscious and the theory of psychoanalytic technique. *The International Journal of Psychoanalysis, 100*, 1068–1083. DOI: 10.1080/00207578.2019.1622425

United Nations. (Retrieved June 21, 2021). *Ending poverty.* https://www.un.org/en/global-issues/ending-poverty

U.S. Census Bureau. (Retrieved June 19, 2021). https://www.census.gov/library/publications/2019/demo/p60–266.html

U.S. Commission on Civil Rights. (2019). *Beyond suspensions: Examining school discipline policies and connections to the school to prison pipeline for students of color with disabilities.* https://www.usccr.gov/pubs/2019/07–23–Beyond-Suspensions.pdf

U.S. Department of Education. (2018). *Individuals with Disabilities Education Act.* https://sites.ed.gov/idea/regs/b/a/300.8/c/10

Vaughan, F. (2003). What is spiritual intelligence? *Journal of Humanistic Psychology, 42*, 16–33.

Voulgarides, C. K., & Tefera, A. (2017). Reframing the racialization of disability in policy. *Theory into Practice, 56*, 161–168.

Voulgarides, C. K., Fergus, E., & Torius, K. A. K. (2017). Pursuing equity: Disproportionality in special education and the reframing of technical solutions to address systematic inequities. *Review of Research in Education, 41*, 61–87.

Vygotsky, L. S. (1962). *Thought and language.* MIT Press.

Wallas, G. (1926). *The art of thought.* Harcourt, Brace, & World.

Weaver, C. (2009). *Reading process.* Heinemann.

Werker, J. E., & Teres, R. C. (1999). Influences on infant speech processing: Toward a new synthesis. *Annual Review of Psychology, 50*, 509–535.

Wilkerson, I. (2020). *Caste: The origins of our discontents.* Random House.

Wurdinger, S. (2005). *Using experiential learning in the classroom: Practical ideas for all educators.* ScareCrow Education.

X, M., & Haley, A. (1965). *The autobiography of Malcom X.* Grove Press.

Zeichner, K. M., & Liston, D. P. (1996). *Reflective teaching: An introduction.* Lawrence Erlbaum Associates.

Zhang, D., & Katsiyannis, A. (2020). Minority representation ins special education: A persistent challenge. *Remedial and Special Education, 23,* 180–187.

Zhang, D., Katsiyannis, A., Ju, S., & Roberts, E. (2014). Minority representation in special education: 5–year trends. *Journal of Child and Family Studies, 23,* 118–127.

Zohar, D., & Marshall, I. (2000). *Connecting with our spiritual intelligence.* Bloomsbury Publishing.

Index

About the Author

Dr. Andrew P. Johnson is Professor of Literacy Instruction and Distinguished Faculty Scholar at Minnesota State University, Mankato. After teaching in the elementary classroom for 9 years, he received a PhD from the University of Minnesota in Literacy Instruction in 1997. He has been working in higher education for 26 years. He is the author of 14 books and over 50 book chapters and academic articles related to literacy, learning, and the human condition. He is also the host of the podcast *The Reading Instruction Show* at https://rss.com/podcasts/drandy. He lives in Mankato, Minnesota, with his wife, Dr. Nancy Fitzsimons, and their two dogs, Emmett and Sasha.

www.ingramcontent.com/pod-product-compliance
Lightning Source LLC
Chambersburg PA
CBHW030647270326
41929CB00007B/245